ASIA

SEA

RED SEA

MOZAMBIQUE CHANNEL

AUSTRALIA

INDIAN   OCEAN

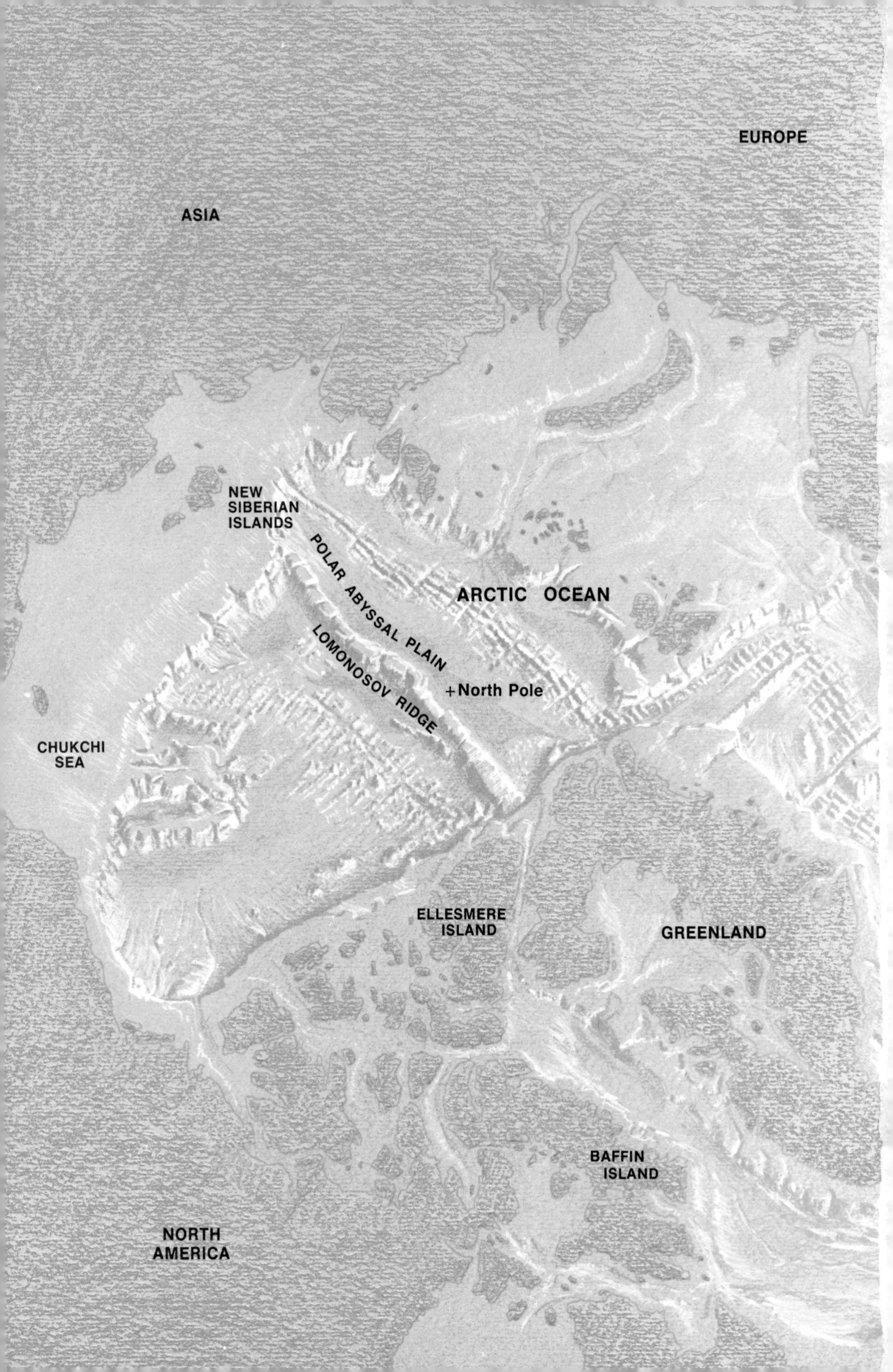

EUROPE

ASIA

NEW
SIBERIAN
ISLANDS

POLAR ABYSSAL PLAIN

ARCTIC OCEAN

LOMONOSOV RIDGE

+North Pole

CHUKCHI
SEA

ELLESMERE
ISLAND

GREENLAND

BAFFIN
ISLAND

NORTH
AMERICA

THE

*Like beckoning fingers, tube sponges cluster on a coral reef in the
Caribbean Sea. This delicate marine ecosystem, one small
kingdom in the vast ocean realm, teems with incredible life.*

DAVID DOUBILET

OCEAN REALM

Prepared by the Special Publications Division
National Geographic Society, Washington, D. C.

The Ocean Realm

Robert D. Ballard, Linda McCarter Bridge,
Sylvia A. Earle, Tee Loftin, Joseph B.
MacInnis, Tom Melham, H. Robert Morrison,
Contributing Authors

Published by
The National Geographic Society
Robert E. Doyle, *President*
Melvin M. Payne, *Chairman of the Board*
Gilbert M. Grosvenor, *Editor*
Melville Bell Grosvenor, *Editor Emeritus*

Prepared by
The Special Publications Division
Robert L. Breeden, *Editor*
Donald J. Crump, *Associate Editor*
Philip B. Silcott, *Senior Editor*
William R. Gray, *Managing Editor*
Toni Eugene, Patricia F. Frakes, *Research*
Annmarie Manzi, *Research Assistant*

Illustrations and Design
Thomas B. Powell, III, *Picture Editor*
Jody Bolt, *Art Director*
Suez B. Kehl, *Assistant Art Director*
Thomas Bolt, Linda McCarter Bridge,
    Christine K. Eckstrom, Judith S. Green,
    Louis de la Haba, James H. Mooney,
    Picture Legends
John D. Garst, Jr., Margaret A. Deane,
    Alfred L. Zebarth, *Map Research and
    Production*

Production and Printing
Robert W. Messer, *Production Manager*
George V. White, *Assistant Production Manager*
Raja D. Murshed, June L. Graham,
    Christine A. Roberts, David V. Showers,
    Production Assistants
Debra A. Antonini, Barbara Bricks, Jane
    H. Buxton, Rosamund Garner, Suzanne
    J. Jacobson, Cleo Petroff, Katheryn M.
    Slocum, Suzanne Venino, *Staff Assistants*
Barbara L. Klein, *Index*

*Bull sea lion nestles with a cow—one of
his harem of several—and a bellowing
pup along the coast of Argentina.*

*Page 1: Tentacle extended, a six-inch-long
octopus, one of an endless parade of
creatures in the ocean, scoots along the
sandy bottom off California. Endpapers:
Maps of the ocean floors. Hardcover
design: A foot-long lionfish in the Red Sea
bristles with poison-charged spines.*

4

*Spike-finned and fierce-
looking, a brightly hued
Irish Lord scouts the rocky
seafloor off the coast of
British Columbia. The foot-
long fish searches for crabs,
mussels, and barnacles.*

NEIL G. MCDANIEL, OCEAN IMAGES

THE

Storm clouds roil above the Gulf of Mexico as moisture drawn from the sea returns as rain. Beneath the waves lies the rich and varied life of the ocean realm, a vast and fragile wilderness.

DAVID DOUBILET

CALL OF THE SEA
An Introduction

By Sylvia A. Earle

TOM MYERS (ABOVE); GINI KELLOGG, SEA LIBRARY (BELOW); DAVID DOUBILET

Avalanche of foam tumbles from the crest of a 20-foot storm wave as it plunges against the rocky coast of California. From booming surf to quiet depths, winds and currents churn the world's ocean—actually one immense interlocking sea. A sand fall (below, left) cascades through a submarine canyon in Pacific Ocean waters off Baja California. Like palm trees bowed in a gale, flexible corals known as gorgonians (below) sway in a surge off the Bahamas. A network of currents flows through the ocean, intermixing polar and tropical waters and circulating nutrients throughout the sea.

Sparkles of sunlight danced on emerald water as I prepared to plunge, for the first time, into what I consider the most incredible wilderness on earth—the ocean realm. I had long yearned for this moment, and now, at age 17, my wish was being fulfilled. Excitement and apprehension surged through me as I strapped on my scuba gear and balanced on the stern of a boat that floated lightly in the Gulf of Mexico just five miles off northwestern Florida. I took a deep breath and jumped, and that jump changed my life forever.

In the thousands of hours I have since spent underwater, I have always experienced the same sensations of joy, freedom, discovery, and love for a spellbinding wilderness that I felt on that first dive.

Initially, though, I was somewhat confused—my breath came too fast; I swallowed some water. Then, miraculously it seemed, compressed air filled my lungs. I exhaled and watched a galaxy of silver bubbles chase each other upward. A gold and brown triggerfish swept past my face mask, and I followed it through a meadow of swaying turtle grass. I glided past a cluster of sponges and touched a silky red plant growing on a rock. Effortlessly, I stood on one finger, enjoying the sensation of weightlessness. I rolled over and looked at the surface shimmering like glass 15 feet overhead. When it was finally time to return to the boat, I knew that I had found a second home.

Almost anyone can experience what I did, discovering a world of unparalleled beauty by slipping over the side of a boat. The moods, the splendor, the diversity of the sea are infinite—towering mountains and jet-black trenches, delicate plants and fierce predators, microscopic diatoms and gigantic whales. The ocean is the caldron where life originated, and it retains much of its elemental character. Creatures exist whose heritage precedes ours by millions of years, and to whom we are as alien as visitors from space. Ironically, if we are to enter their world for more than a few moments, we must backtrack through evolution and sprout steel "gills."

More than a century and a half ago, the English poet Lord Byron wrote of the sea:

"Roll on, thou deep and dark blue Ocean—roll!
Ten thousand fleets sweep over thee in vain;
Man marks the earth with ruin—his control
Stops with the shore."

Today, much of that ocean still remains untamed and untouched. But change, inevitably, has come. The sea is now marked, as the land and air are marked, with the imprint of human ways. In two centuries, earth's population has quintupled and has overtaken much of the wilderness land. Forest, desert, plain, and even tundra have yielded to city and town, farm and factory. Ships larger than some towns of Byron's time commute among the continents, cruising the surface of what remains—in many remarkable ways—a virtual wilderness. *(Continued on page 20)*

Sunlight dapples shallows off Chincoteague Island in Virginia as a motionless great blue heron surveys the water for fish. Haven for land and sea creatures alike, such protected regions as beaches, bays, salt marshes, and mangrove swamps harbor nutrient-rich waters that nourish myriad plants and animals. These fertile shallows that rim the ocean serve as nurseries for many species of marine life.

NATIONAL GEOGRAPHIC PHOTOGRAPHER
BATES LITTLEHALES

Bold as their color, garibaldis dart like orange flames along the rocky floor of a giant-kelp forest off the coast of southern California. Curious but fiercely territorial, the "goldfish of the sea" (right) will abruptly nudge intruders that venture too close to their nests—or follow divers exploring the tangled kelp beds. "Garibaldis have amazing character and personality," says author Sylvia A. Earle. "They stay with you and pester you. I often wonder what they're seeing—and who is watching whom!" Conspicuous in the green-brown world of the kelp forest, the foot-long garibaldis, now protected by law in California, rely on aggressive behavior to frighten their enemies. Submarine jungles of giant kelp, flourishing in cool coastal waters off Pacific North America, shelter a treasure trove of sea creatures. Many kelp dwellers rely on camouflage for survival, blending with the fronds of this fast-growing plant. Snails and crabs graze along the swaying blades, and several species of sea stars move among the kelp plants to feed and breed. Rivaling the garibaldi's vivid hue, two blood sea stars (below) stand on tiptoe to spawn in the secluded shadows of a kelp forest floor.

TOM MYERS (UPPER); HOWARD HALL (LOWER); JACK MCKENNEY

Silvery burst of glassy sweepers veils the entrance to a cave in the Red Sea as a diver kicks to the surface for air. As if soaring on undersea winds, a sea lion (above) frolics off the Galapagos Islands in the Pacific. The flippers of this marine mammal evolved from terrestrial limbs; fossil evidence reveals that its ancestors once lived on land. Sea lions remain partially bound to the shore, where they sun, sleep, and bear their young. Streamlined for life in the sea, a dolphin (below)—another mammal—sails through Atlantic waters. Though no longer tied to land, dolphins, like sea lions, evolved from creatures that once lived ashore. With diving gear, man now visits the ocean kingdom. Overleaf: Swirling hurricane of fish, a school of grunts streams through Galapagos waters, a region the author calls "the fishiest place in the world."

CARL ROESSLER, SEA LIBRARY (ABOVE); AL GIDDINGS, SEA FILMS, INC. (BELOW); DAVID DOUBILET (LEFT AND OVERLEAF)

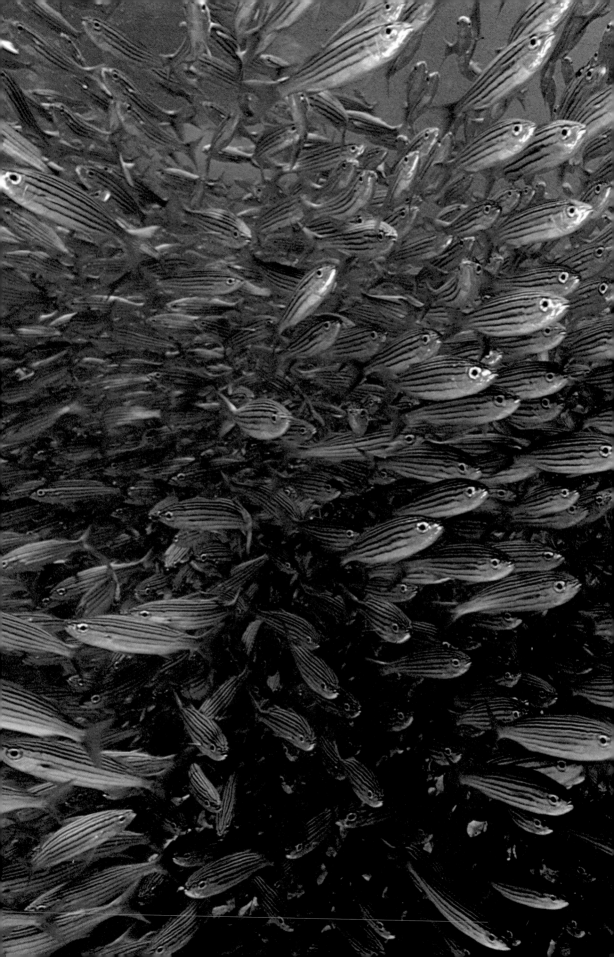

A baseline that makes it possible to measure a century of change in the oceans was established when the British research vessel *Challenger* embarked in 1872 on a scientific circumnavigation. The scientists aboard were the first to probe ocean waters worldwide, to determine the breadth and depth of the sea wilderness, to look for the special plants and animals that live there, and to seek the dimensions and causes of currents, tides, and temperatures. After two million or more years of existence, man was recognizing the sea as something more than an avenue for transportation, a battlefield, a source of storms, an inspiration for poetry, a place where fish are caught.

Government instructions to the *Challenger*'s captain read: ". . . you have been abundantly supplied with all the instruments and apparatus which modern science and practical experience have been able to suggest and devise . . . you have a wide field and virgin ground before you."

To an ecology class, I once tried to explain the difficulties that faced the *Challenger*'s scientists. "Try to imagine," I told them, "that you're flying over a fogbound forest in a slow-moving blimp. You can't see the ground, but an instrument tells you that it is about 3,000 feet down. You don't know exactly where you are, so the chances of returning to the same place twice are slim. To get some idea of what the forest below is like, you drop a line with a basket attached, then tow the basket behind you and hope it will not get snagged or broken. After a while, you pull it up; you're thankful for anything that has been snared—a rock, a twig, a bewildered mouse."

Despite the limitations they faced, the scientists aboard the *Challenger* helped find answers to questions of deceptive simplicity, the sort a child might ask, but scientists then could not answer.

How deep is the sea? No one really knew. But long before echo-sounding and seismic techniques were devised for determining depth, soundings were made from *Challenger*'s decks using the time-honored method of dangling a weight on a calibrated line—a long and laborious process. These soundings established rough contours for the ocean bottom and plumbed the deepest depth then known—26,850 feet, in the western Pacific Ocean.

Do animals live at great depths? Scientists were still not sure, despite disquieting discoveries of strange creatures found in deep-sea dredges or clinging to telegraph cables recovered from thousands of feet down.

During their three and a half years of exploration, *Challenger* scientists collected tens of thousands of fishes and invertebrates. Their research proved not only that animal life is abundant in the deep sea but also that it includes species of relatively recent origin. Some 700 genera and several thousand species new to science tumbled out of *Challenger*'s nets, trawls, and dredges.

Prisoner in a coral castle, a female gall crab lives within a bulblike chamber cupped by branches of needle coral. To survive in the competitive world of Australia's Great Barrier Reef, the young gall crab nestles on a live coral branch, stimulating its stony fingers to grow and encase her. Safe from predators there, the quarter-inch-wide crab filters food from the water. She never leaves her home, but males enter and newly hatched young depart.

Charles Wyville Thomson, chief scientist of the expedition and a widely respected biologist, once believed that the enormous pressure at great depths would be sufficient to rule out any possibility of life in the deep. "There was a curious popular notion," he wrote, "in which I well remember sharing when a boy, that, in going down, the sea-water became gradually under the pressure heavier and heavier, and that all the loose things in the sea floated at different levels, according to their specific weight: skeletons of men, anchors and shot and cannon, and last of all the broad gold pieces wrecked in the loss of many a galleon on the Spanish Main; the whole forming a kind of 'false bottom' to the ocean, beneath which there lay all the depth of clear still water, which was heavier than molten gold."

Thomson later learned that water is virtually incompressible, that density varies little even at the greatest depths, although the sheer weight of water does exert enormous pressure—a phenomenon that divers quickly feel in the air spaces of their ears.

Recent investigations have shown that the diversity of life in some communities at 14,000 feet is roughly equivalent to that in shallow tropical waters. In 1960 the bathyscaph *Trieste* descended to the deepest part of the deepest hole in the deepest trench in the sea—nearly seven miles down in the Challenger Deep. Jacques Piccard, one of two men aboard, later observed, ". . . as we were settling this final fathom, I saw a wonderful thing. Lying on the bottom just beneath us was some type of flatfish, resembling a sole, about 1 foot long and 6 inches across. Even as I saw him, his two round eyes on top of his head spied us—a monster of steel—invading his silent realm." Can life exist in the greatest depths of the ocean? Repeatedly, we have found the answer to be an unequivocal yes.

No human has ever swum free in the deep sea, but I once experienced something of what it must be like to float among the bizarre creatures at those depths. Noted underwater filmmaker Al Giddings invited me to accompany him on a night dive as deep as we could go on compressed air off Grande Comore, an island in the Indian Ocean off Africa. We were part of a California Academy of Sciences expedition organized to observe and to capture a live coelacanth, a fish long believed to be extinct—until a live one was discovered in 1938. Since then, local fishermen have caught nearly a hundred, always in fairly deep water, and always at night. So it seemed reasonable for us to begin our search for coelacanths at night, too.

Al and I jumped from the deck of a small boat into the dark waters of the Mozambique Channel late one moonless night. As we descended past 100 feet, we began to see flickering blue-green lights, like eerie underwater fireflies. We quietly approached one small beacon. Just inches from it, Al switched on his flashlight. Momentarily, a tiny gray fish—a *Photoblepharon*—hung suspended, dazzled by our larger

Wavy volute extends a large muscular foot to walk along the sandy seafloor off the coast of southern Australia. When volutes emerge from the sand at night to feed, the six-inch-long animals reveal the delicate red whorls that pattern their bodies as well as their shells. "The creature inside is often more beautiful than the outer shell that collectors prize so highly," says Sylvia Earle.

beacon. Under each eye, this little "flashlight fish" has a brilliant patch of glowing bacteria that can be revealed or shut off by flicking a lid.

Many creatures of the deep have such luminescent spots, sometimes in rows, and I had often tried to imagine how it would feel to be in their midst. At 200 feet, not 2,000, I found out. I became part of a starburst of lights that sparkled as hundreds of small fish moved overhead in search of food—or one another.

What causes ocean currents, and where do they go? Until the *Challenger* expedition, no one had sampled currents widely using consistent methods—although currents have probably been recognized by sailors as long as ships have plied the sea. Benjamin Franklin, in one of his wide-ranging areas of study, investigated the extent of the Gulf Stream and revealed its influence on sailing time across the North Atlantic Ocean. In due course, it was discovered that the Gulf Stream exerts a warming influence on the climate of Europe as it sweeps close to that continent's northwest coast.

The bond between the sea and daily weather—as well as long-range climate changes—is now fully recognized. But we are still seeking to define patterns of ocean circulation and to predict weather accurately. We do know that the atmosphere drives the ocean, and that the ocean in turn yields energy back to the atmosphere—in a continuous cycle of immense interacting forces.

The sea is always in motion, stirred by earth's spinning, swept by winds, responding to differences of temperature and salinity, influenced by the gravitational tugs of the sun and the moon. According to legend, a despondent Aristotle leaped into the sea and drowned because of his inability to make sense of that kind of water motion called tides. It is easy to appreciate his frustration, knowing as we do now the many factors that cause tides to happen and *not* to happen according to predictions. If the earth were smooth, quiet, and uniformly covered with water, some regularity could be expected. As it is, the configuration of the land and the unruly forces of the wind complicate the rhythms created by the earth's own motions and the gravitational pull of the sun and the moon.

Why is the sea salty? Scientists aboard the *Challenger* could not fully answer the question, but they thoroughly studied 77 samples of seawater. Results verified previous research, showing that the components of marine salt occur in the same proportion worldwide, and that the average salinity of the ocean is about 3.5 percent.

As a small child, I read a Norse yarn about a magic salt mill that was thrown into the sea by a young man who had forgotten how to make the mill stop. According to the story, the mill is there to this day, grinding out the salt that keeps the ocean briny. Later, as a student, I was taught that salt entered the sea gradually as minerals were washed from the land during great deluges early in earth's history.

SUZI GURLEY

Startlingly unexpected life forms inhabit the world's ocean, where some animals resemble plants, some plants look like animals, and color often belies a creature's identity. Above, a bouquet of purple coral— actually an animal in shrubby disguise—lives off the California coast. Primitive animals, orange hydroids (opposite, upper) entwine the crimson branches of a coralline alga. Pigments in this alga mask the presence of chlorophyll, which greens most plants, such as the alga Caulerpa *(opposite, lower).*

Now I'm discovering that what I thought to be truth is overshadowed by an element of reality in the old legend. Salt is being added to the sea from an ocean floor "mill." That mill, as explained by present geophysical theorists, is the 40,000-mile-long midocean rift that extends through the ocean basins. In regions where the seafloor is spreading, basalt—black volcanic rock—flows up through the rift. Along with it comes a liquid called "juvenile" water; it contains many of the salts found in seawater. More juvenile water, with somewhat different elements, is released by submarine volcanoes. Not only much of the salt but also the actual water that fills the ocean may have come from these sources.

Earth, alone, in our entire solar system, is blessed with abundant water. Mercury is too small and too hot to support an ocean. Venus, also, is hot and nearly waterless. Mars has traces of water vapor and possibly some ice at the poles, but no water available in the liquid form necessary for life as we know it. The outer planets lack the conditions to have water in the liquid state. Our small planet has just the right combination of such factors as composition and distance from the sun to produce and to retain water in all of its three states: ice, vapor, and, most important, liquid.

However, earth might have no ocean if it were not for one peculiarity—water is most dense just before it freezes. Ice therefore floats on the surface instead of sinking to the bottom. If conditions were otherwise, rivers, lakes, and even the sea itself would freeze solid from the bottom up. As it is, the ice that floats on the surface insulates the water below, allowing it to stay in liquid form.

Of all the water that exists on earth—some 326,000,000 cubic miles—less than 3 percent is fresh, and most of that is locked into icecaps and glaciers. Rain has its origin, for the most part, in the sea. Some four-fifths of the water that evaporates into the atmosphere each year comes from the ocean. And the ocean re-collects most of that again when it falls as rain or snow.

Scientists believe that the majority of earth's plant and animal species are land-based, although they occupy only about 30 percent of the world's area. Yet all of the 25 or so great divisions of animals—and most of the divisions of plants—are represented in the sea. More than half of these divisions are found only in a marine environment.

Will we discover, as we explore further, that the greatest diversity of organisms is, in fact, aquatic? Sound reasons have been proposed to account for the presence of fewer species in the sea than on land, but our terrestrial bias may have influenced this conclusion. When entire undersea mountain ranges escape notice, as they did until only a few decades ago, it seems reasonable to assume that there are numerous marine habitats and inhabitants that we have yet to encounter.

We have left footprints on the moon, but none yet mark

the deepest ocean floor. Submarines, like space vehicles, have transported observers to places once unreachable, and with cameras we have glimpsed things we have not yet touched. With much help from modern technology, a few humans have experienced the pressure of the sea on their bodies at more than 1,000 feet. But relying only on lung power, face mask, flippers, and weights, it is nearly impossible for a diver to go below 250 feet. Basically, we are terrestrial beings, with no special adaptations that make us suited for an aquatic existence—even as short-term visitors—except our brains and our toolmaking ability.

For two thousand years, the *ama*, women divers of Japan, have dived into the sea to gather food. Few go deeper than 75 feet, and seldom does a dive last more than 90 seconds. A hunter on land, if limited to 90-second excursions into the forest while holding his breath, would be hard-pressed to return with a kill. Explorers in the sea are confronted with similar restrictions. The wonder is not that the sea is a wilderness to humans, but that we have come to know as much as we do considering the obstacles.

I overcame some of those obstacles in 1975 to explore the vertical drop-off that borders a broad, steep-sided ocean bowl in the Bahamas named Tongue of the Ocean. I joined three companions for a week 60 feet underwater in Hydro-Lab, a one-room laboratory-bunkhouse-galley that provided far less space to each of us than was available to scientists aboard the *Challenger*. But we did have access to the sea with the perspective of a resident.

On my first visit to the drop-off, I glided silently through clear, deep-blue water, nearly mesmerized by the beauty surrounding me. At 250 feet down, I hung suspended above more than a thousand feet of ocean wilderness. I responded to a powerful human force—curiosity—and within minutes experienced one of the greatest of human pleasures—discovery.

I found a miniature forest of velvety, disk-shaped plants carpeting a narrow ledge. My excitement mounted as I watched these tiny green plants sway gently in the current and tried to catalog them in my mind. I knew that I had never seen them before, and I couldn't place them in any of the many marine botany books I had read. I had a hunch and later confirmed it—I had discovered a species of algae hitherto unknown to mankind.

On many dives, I feel as if I am an other-world intruder as I cruise around coral reefs, selecting a few plants for specimens. Surprisingly, I draw little attention most of the time. Sometimes, though, persistent individuals or even whole schools of fish come my way and follow me around. Once, near Hydro-Lab, I noticed the sleek silver forms of some local citizens circling overhead. With great grace they spiraled toward me, more than a hundred horse-eye jacks flowing as one. Almost immediately, I was surrounded, some individuals passing so close that I felt their motion through the water. Their eyes met my eyes, and perhaps some information registered on both sides before they passed on, returning to the water-sky above me.

More recently, I approached a spiny lobster on a grassy underwater slope off the island of San Salvador, one of the Bahamas. With some effort, I put aside thoughts of lemon slices and melted butter, and experienced a memorable encounter. Perhaps because I moved very slowly and breathed as quietly as I could, the lobster stayed where he was and allowed me to approach to within just a few inches of his long-spined antennae. I stopped then, lying among the long

NASA

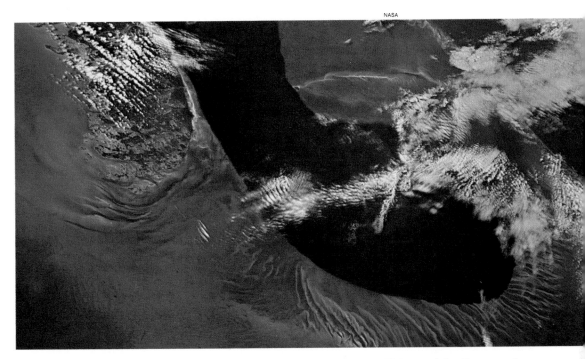

blades of turtle grass, and looked at a lobster as I had never looked at a lobster before. Those shiny black compound eyes—what were they seeing? Multiple images? One composite me?

As I mused, the lobster began moving toward me, armored legs lifting, bending. Very gently, his two long outer antennae touched the edge of my face plate. I heard soft whirring noises, saw eyestalks tilt slightly. Who, I wondered, is watching whom? Would I be so bold and stand my ground if I were approached by a creature as large and unfamiliar to me as I must be to this small lobster?

I often try to imagine what the reaction would be if a creature twenty times human size landed in downtown Washington, D. C., and moved quietly around, picking up a shrub here, a tree there, perhaps scooping up a few people and putting them in a sack before gliding off to some strange and different world.

We humans are recent arrivals on earth, and still come

Tongue of the Ocean, a deep-blue abyss in the Great Bahama Bank, curves past the eastern shore of Andros Island in a photograph taken 105 miles up by Apollo 9 astronauts. Turquoise shallows rim the 40-mile-wide bowl at the tip of the Tongue. In places the Tongue drops a mile or more to the bottom of the Atlantic.

25

as visitors underwater. Our origin is there—as is the origin of living things in general. But fish have existed for more than 400 million years, whales for some 50 million. Lobster relatives have lived in sea crevices for nearly half a billion years. The first primates called humans evolved only a couple of million years ago.

I am not sure what would most astonish Charles Wyville Thomson and his *Challenger* colleagues about the discoveries made since their day. Continental drift? Subsea mountain ranges? Nuclear power? Genetic codes? The view of earth from space? The ability to breathe underwater? Submersibles? Electron microscopes?

Or would it be something more general, perhaps the awareness that the sea is not limitless or immutable, indeed that it has changed noticeably in a mere hundred years?

In one century, we have come to know more about the sea than we learned during all preceding history. We now understand that the ocean influences the broad cycles of climate and weather, that it absorbs most of the sunlight that strikes the earth and creates most of the oxygen we breathe, that it absorbs huge amounts of carbon dioxide, and that it is the source of most fresh water.

The ocean realm, as viewed with our newfound knowledge, is a continuous, interlocking sea—one, not seven as old sea stories suggested. But even more than that, the sea merges with the atmosphere, and both join with the land as a single, dynamic system. Astronauts have given us a comprehensive view of our planet that makes this concept more believable, somehow, than was possible from our previous earthbound perspective.

Geologists, with their magnificent feel for time on a grand scale, show us how restless the sea really is, changing shape and size many times in just a billion years. To them, the Atlantic Ocean is fairly young, only about 150 million years of age. The Red Sea is infantile. And the Mediterranean Sea, which today faces possible ecological peril, completely dried up not long ago, geologically speaking.

Also geologically speaking, we humans are virtual newcomers. However, measured in time units that matter to us—lifetimes—we are causing changes that approach the geological in magnitude. We join by canals waters that have been separated for millions of years. We create dry land out of seafloor and carve harbors from marshlands that were tens of thousands of years in the making. In a matter of just a few decades, we have inadvertently spread films of oil and chemicals upon the very surface that supplies life-giving oxygen and fresh water.

One of the most significant things learned in this century, I believe, is the importance of the sea to our well-being and survival, the necessity of an ocean wilderness to the health of the world's environment. We have learned that the ocean greatly affects all living things, from deep-sea fish to desert mouse.

SYLVIA A. EARLE

Taxi to the depths, a submersible descends slowly into the Tongue of the Ocean. In 1975, it shuttled Sylvia Earle and three companions from a laboratory-habitat 60 feet undersea to the dark domain far below. Seeking clues to how plants and animals survive at depth, the divers explored the steep wall of the Tongue— and discovered previously unknown species of seaweed and coral.

We also know that we have set in motion cycles that may drastically alter the ocean as we know it today. The ocean realm is vast and diverse—but also fragile. Oil spills, overfishing, dumping of garbage, chemicals, and radioactive substances have all diminished the health of the ocean. But much of the wilderness character of a century ago remains, and with care and an understanding of the value of the sea, that character can be preserved.

In the pages of this book you will find words and photographs that evoke the beauty of the ocean realm. Each chapter is illustrated with the artistry of many who not only have been at the right place at the right time with the right camera, but who also have the eye and the experience to recognize the extraordinary.

Less than a century ago, the first underwater photograph had not been taken. Fifty years ago, the most ordinary picture by today's standards would have astonished people. This volume contains the work of many people who are rightfully regarded as exceptional in the art of underwater photography. Among them are Bill Curtsinger, David Doubilet, Douglas Faulkner, and Al Giddings.

They, and the other photographers whose work is shown here, have contended with, and found solutions to, problems of lighting—red and yellow are completely absorbed in the top dozen yards of even the clearest seawater; leaking—under pressure, water quickly penetrates any opening in an air-filled camera housing; and the distortions brought about in an aquatic medium. Each, artistically, has provided eyes in the sea for all of us.

In the first chapter author H. Robert Morrison surveys highly productive waters along the shallow shores—salt marshes and mangrove swamps, sea-grass meadows and sand beaches, and then looks outward to the edges of the continental shelf. In many of these shallow areas, fresh water mixes with salt, and life forms from the ocean intermingle with those closer to land. Because of their proximity to land, bays, estuaries, and marshes are perhaps most familiar to people. But they, and the adjacent continental shelf areas, are also more vulnerable to damage.

Linda McCarter Bridge explores cold, rocky shores in the second chapter. She submerged in underwater forests of kelp and found the nutrient-rich currents that have given rise to some of the world's great fisheries. She dived with sea otters and came eye to eye with an octopus.

Tom Melham, in the next chapter, captures the beauty of coral reefs. He visited several coral areas in a few months' time—an accomplishment that would have astounded scientists in Lord Byron's day. No *Challenger* scientist could ever have hoped to see what Melham saw—underwater views of the Red Sea, the Caribbean Sea, the South Pacific, and the Great Barrier Reef off the coast of Australia.

Some of the most intricate   (Continued on page 32)

Overleaf: Humpback whales slip through violet waters off the island of Maui in Hawaii. Lithe and graceful despite their awesome size, humpbacks steer underwater with long winglike flippers—and slap them on the surface with playful zest. "The name humpback seems most unfortunate for such a beautiful creature," says Sylvia Earle, who has dived with the giants off Alaska and Hawaii. "It suggests something awkward or ponderous, and they are not that at all. They are more like seabirds underwater. They glide and flow with the grace of swallows."

SYLVIA A. EARLE, SEA FILMS, INC. (OVERLEAF)

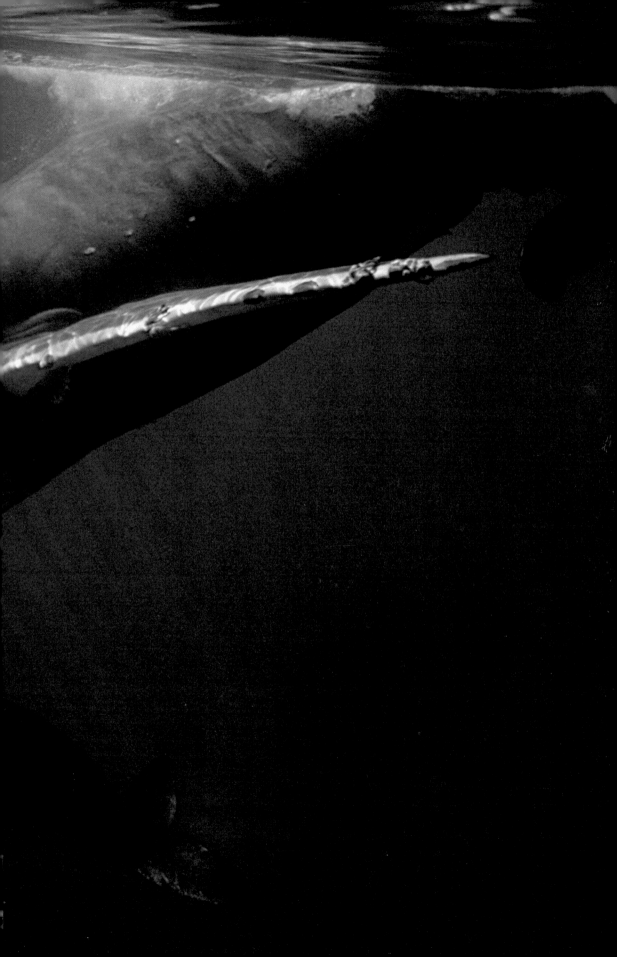

*Blizzard of Aurelia jellyfish swarms past Sylvia
Earle as she dives in the warm Pacific waters of
Truk Lagoon. "I jumped in and found these jewels
floating by," she recalled. "They swept over me in
a billowing cloud, millions of them. Then, just as
suddenly, they were gone." Pushed by currents
and winds, jellyfish swim slowly through the sea
by tensing and relaxing muscles in their bell-
shaped bodies. Buoyed by a translucent layer of
gel, a Polyorchis jellyfish (left) glides toward the
surface of San Francisco Bay. A sleek squid
(below) jets through a channel in the Great Barrier
Reef. Like a chameleon, the squid changes color
and pattern in less than a second to merge with its
surroundings. Beyond reach of the sun, creatures
of the depths—a red shrimp (bottom, right) and a
hatchetfish (bottom, left)—survive in a world of
chilling darkness and tremendous pressure.*

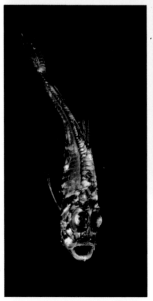

strategies for survival in the world are acted out on coral reefs—from fish with poisonous spines to crabs that build castles of coral. Animals are most conspicuous here: fishes, sponges, mollusks, and dozens of different corals. Less conspicuous but often more abundant are the hundreds of plants that grow within and around the corals. Two-thirds of the living material on a reef, in fact, may be plant tissue.

To many people, coral reefs are comparable to human works of art in their grace and beauty. But several wilderness reef areas, including the Palau Islands in the Pacific, are being considered as sites for oil ports—a destiny few would condone were the Louvre at stake.

Like tourists on a crowded ferry, Adélie penguins ride a cake of sea ice through Antarctic waters. Wholly dependent on the ocean for food, penguins swim undersea with flippers—modified wings—in search of crustaceans. In the numbing cold, their familiar tuxedos—feathers as dense and waterproof as fur—offer both protection and camouflage. Seen from above, their backs blend with the dark sea; from below, their white bellies match the sunlit surface.

Tee Loftin is a newcomer to the exploration of the ocean and, as such, has a special message for all who encounter the sea for the first time. In her chapter, she looks at perhaps the most awesome of all the ocean arenas, the open waters beyond sight of land.

Minute jewel-like drifters, migrating turtles, and predators such as sharks and tuna populate the open sea. Imagine with her the sensation of floating in the middle of the ocean, infinite blue above and below, where calms and storms are born, where air and sea become one. Travel to the Galapagos Islands, where several species of birds, lizards, and mammals have partially returned to the sea.

While Tee Loftin looks at the tips of the mountains that break the surface as the Galapagos Islands, geologist Robert D. Ballard goes 10,000 feet down, to the base of the same mountains. In small submersibles, Dr. Ballard descends with the rain of nutrients that continuously falls to the dark seafloor. There he encounters life forms that have developed under unimaginable conditions of cold, darkness, and pressure. Discover with him rare hot-water seeps where, in the absence of light, bacteria, instead of green plants, provide the basic energy for an unusual food web.

To me, the deep sea traditionally meant that never-never land inhabited by luminous gelatinous creatures, bizarre black fish, and brilliant red shrimp. But Dr. Ballard also shows how even the deepest ocean bottom is related to all other parts of the ocean realm.

Some people view the deep sea as a safe place to deposit nuclear wastes and other dangerous material. It is becoming increasingly apparent that such disposal is not simply a problem for future generations, but a matter of haunting concern today.

In the final chapter, explore beneath the ice of both the Arctic and Antarctic with undersea medical pioneer Joseph

B. MacInnis. Discover the unique ways that plants and animals have adapted to life in these frigid waters. The polar seas are fragile and delicately balanced. Once disturbed, that balance is difficult to restore.

There is much talk, for instance, of tapping the enormous freshwater resource locked in polar ice, of towing icebergs to arid lands. There is *little* talk of how this might affect life at the poles, or of how large-scale ice removal might affect weather and thermal cycles around the world.

Why is there a need to protect the sea, or even to be concerned about the health or future of it? Why should people, especially those who do not live by the sea, care if there is an occasional oil spill?

The answer is rooted in the awareness that we all live "by the sea." We depend on the sea for an environmental stability that we have always taken for granted, simply because we always *could* take it for granted.

Now, while threats to that stability are still mostly potential and while the sea is still reasonably healthy, we must establish precedents that will ensure the survival of the wilderness ocean realm.

In so doing, we might well ensure our own.

Overleaf: Tethered by a safety line, a diver wearing an insulated wetsuit dangles weightlessly beneath jumbled Arctic ice. Man has only recently begun to probe the frigid waters of the Arctic Ocean—one of the harshest, most hostile environments of the ocean realm.

JOSEPH B. MACINNIS (OVERLEAF)

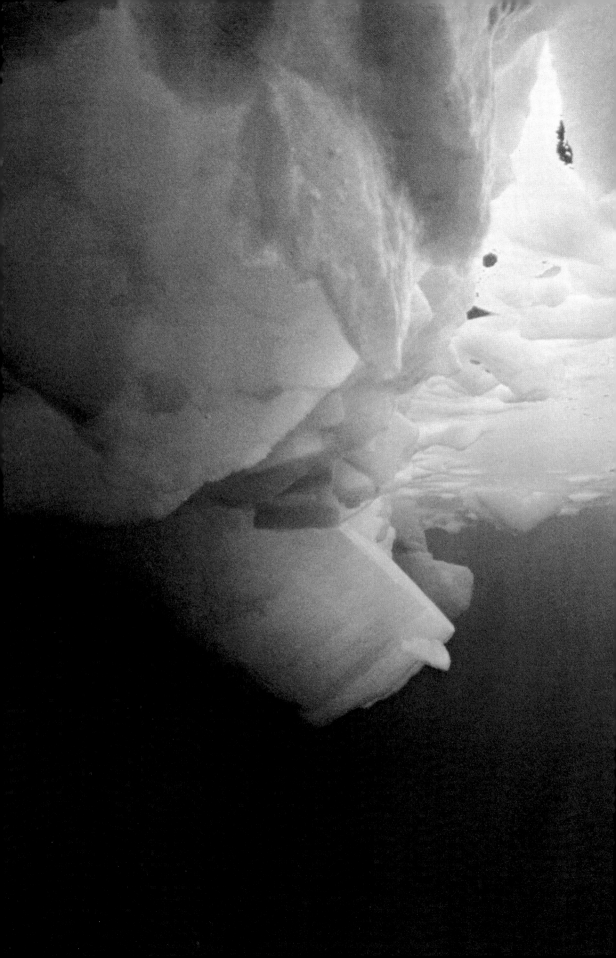

THE

Like stilts, prop roots support a young red mangrove growing in a tranquil bay in the Florida Keys. Such hospitable coastal waters, warm and shallow, nurture a diversity of marine life.

SHALLOW SHORES

By H. Robert Morrison

udden and violent, a roiling thunderstorm swept the small offshore island I was exploring. Its fury lasted only long enough to soak me thoroughly—and then it was gone. But in its wake, it left a breathtaking legacy. The beach, previously crisscrossed by footprints, was now pristine.

Tentatively, I ventured onto the rain-dimpled sand. The only object I could see—except for a few birds wheeling overhead—was a small conch shell uncovered by the storm. I picked it up and brushed away the sand. Immediately I noticed the startling pearly pink color of the shell and felt its unexpected silkiness.

As I studied it, a tiny claw protruded from the shell and slowly, warily, began to probe my hand. Fascinated, I watched a tiny hermit crab extend more appendages until a sudden movement of my hand caused it to snap back into the conch shell, which it used for protection and as a home. After a few moments, I returned it to a small tidal pool, and it soon began crawling about the sandy bottom, lugging along its borrowed house.

This was the first of many quiet but intriguing discoveries I made as I investigated the realm of the shallow shores. My explorations of that realm took me along the southern East Coast of the United States, around the tip of Florida, and into the Gulf of Mexico. I found a diverse world of muddy salt marshes and tangled mangrove swamps—nutrient-rich havens for land and sea creatures alike.

From the fringe of the coastline, these shallow areas yield to the continental shelf, which nurtures myriad marine plants and animals. This shelf often slopes gently downward for dozens of miles before dropping off to the black abyss of the deep.

I began my journeys at Cape Hatteras National Seashore, along the Outer Banks of North Carolina. The evening I arrived, I took a long walk on the beach with my wife, Dottie. We expected to find nearly endless displays of life in these hospitable Atlantic waters. But we saw only a few sea oats waving in the breeze, scattered bits of shell and seaweed on the beach, and some birds flying above the dunes.

Next morning, when we met Clay Gifford, Resources Management Specialist for the seashore, I asked where all the creatures were. "To find the full variety of life in these shallow areas," answered Clay, a wiry man whose tanned face reflects his years in the sun and salt air, "you have to learn a little bit about the creatures and their habits. Mud and sand, you see, give things a place to hide. You have to search out these hiding places—and be patient."

Following Clay's advice, Dottie and I joined Ken John—a young naturalist then with Cape Hatteras National Seashore—on a half-day canoe tour of a nearby salt marsh. As we pushed off into calm shallow waters on an August morning that was already baking hot, he told us something about

salt marshes.

"They're one of the richest, most productive ecological systems in the world. An acre of Iowa farmland, for instance, doesn't produce nearly as much vegetation as an acre of salt marsh, which collects nutrients from the sea as well as from the land.

"The unending supply of decaying matter provides a perfect medium for bacteria and other microorganisms. These tiny bits of life are eaten by the larvae of many different creatures, which are in turn fed on by snails, crabs and other crustaceans, and the young of many fishes. Larger animals are attracted to the salt marsh to feed—and they are fed upon by even larger ones. This entire complex process is called a food web. What begins with dead plant tissue ultimately feeds the largest creatures in the ocean. That's why salt marshes are sometimes called the nurseries of the sea."

After several minutes of quiet paddling, we stopped on a muddy bank lapped by a slowly rising tide. We stepped out of the canoe and walked along the slippery bank. Ken grabbed a leaf of three-foot-high grass.

"This is cordgrass," he explained, "one of the most typical plants found in a marsh. It grows, somehow, partially submerged in salt water. Because of the harsh conditions, only a few kinds of plants can grow at all in salt marshes, and this is one of the most successful." He pointed to droplets glistening on the blades. "This is actually salt water that the plant has exuded. In a couple of hours, as the sun climbs higher, you'll see tiny crystals of salt dried on the blades. This is one process that allows the cordgrass to keep its salinity in balance."

Dottie and I hunkered down as Ken dug into the shallow bottom for a handful of black muck. Thick and rich, it squeezed between his fingers like tacky grease, and emitted the distinct sweet smell of decay. "Rotting marsh grasses, mixed with water, microorganisms, and other decaying material, help produce this mud," Ken explained. "With the incessant stirring of tides, winds, and storms, some of the mud becomes suspended in the water. The salt marsh is thus bathed in a nutrient-rich soup, a near-perfect environment for the young of dozens of species of fishes, crustaceans, and insects."

He slapped at a mosquito, one of several circling his face. "These mosquitoes, for example, grow from larvae that are an important source of food for young fish. So next time a mosquito bites you, just think of it as one step toward your next fillet of flounder dinner."

I dipped down for a scoop of the black mud, and to my surprise pulled up an oyster along with it. With a whoop of excitement, I realized that I had discovered a hiding place, the first since I had talked with Clay Gifford. A few minutes later, Dottie found another—hidden among the blades on a stalk of cordgrass was a snail. "It's a periwinkle," Ken said. "It spends its life crawling up and down the grass, keeping near the waterline as (Continued on page 44)

BOTH BY NATIONAL GEOGRAPHIC PHOTOGRAPHER BIANCA LAVIES

Grasping a mosquito fish, a three-inch-long pink shrimp (opposite) feeds in a mangrove swamp in Florida. Above, a shrimp falls prey in turn to a hermit crab. Hatched by the million from spring through autumn off the Dry Tortugas, the young shrimp travel a hundred miles to Florida's estuaries. There, they mature. In winter, shrimp that have survived predation and fishing nets return to the Dry Tortugas to spawn, completing a life cycle based along the shallow shores.

Tangled tapestry of red mangroves fills the shallows of Rookery Bay in Florida. Mangroves form dense thickets by continuously sending young shoots into new waters. Seedlings also drift on the tides to other shallow areas and form new colonies. At left, a thousand-pound manatee, or sea cow, approaches a mangrove branch. A calf sticks close to its mother. Both will surface about every five minutes to breathe through valved nostrils. Manatees eat as much as a hundred pounds of water plants each day. The U. S. Fish and Wildlife Service has declared the manatee an endangered species. These marine mammals once roamed rivers and coastal waters from Texas to the Carolinas; today not more than a thousand of the creatures survive. Overleaf: Hundreds of tiny fish explode in a thicket of mangrove roots in the Florida Keys. Mangroves trap nutrient-rich sediment from both river and ocean, providing one of the world's most fertile environments.

BOTH AND OVERLEAF BY NATIONAL GEOGRAPHIC PHOTOGRAPHER BIANCA LAVIES

the tide ebbs and flows. It eats algae growing on the stem."

The three of us soon drifted apart, pulled in different directions by different interests. After a few minutes of wandering, I found that I was alone with the sounds of the salt marsh. A gently whispering breeze stirred the cordgrass. Frogs croaked intermittently, punctuating the steady hum of insects. Birds sang, and wavelets slapped gently against the mudbanks. I felt something of the primeval magic that must have existed here in past centuries. Alone, and far from the crowds and clutter of urban centers, I felt a oneness with nature.

I thought with sadness about the miles of coastline already taken over by cities, towns, and factories, about the acres of salt marsh destroyed by dredging, filling, and pollution. I recalled that, according to one estimate, more than a fourth of the nation's coastal saline areas have been destroyed since 1922. A few hundred acres have been rehabilitated, but this process is only in its pioneering stages.

As scientists have made known their findings about the rich productivity of these areas, the Federal Government and a number of state governments have responded with measures limiting the destruction of marshlands. Many besieged wetlands have thus been spared. And, especially for the millions of Americans who live near the shallow shores, there remain opportunities to visit salt marshes and lonely seashores, to experience the wilderness and freedom that exist there.

A rustling sound in the tall grass nearby interrupted my thoughts. An ungainly clapper rail, a gray-brown bird with long legs and a sharp beak, was stalking crabs and insects along a mudbank. Birds, I soon came to realize, are among the principal characters of the shallow shores. Migrating birds use the rich marshlands as resting and feeding areas. It's not uncommon to see dozens of species together in one small salt marsh. I quickly learned to identify some of them: black terns, least terns, short-billed dowitchers, lesser yellowlegs, sandpipers, gulls.

Early one morning, I was exploring a brackish marsh when two dozen shorebirds exploded skyward in a cloud of wings. A moment later, I saw the cause of this sudden activity. Soaring effortlessly above me was a marsh hawk, a predator of small birds, fishes, and mammals. Each time it made a pass, the smaller birds would take flight in alarm. When it flew out of sight, they would slowly settle back to their morning feeding.

On a sunny afternoon, Dottie and I were walking along the beach watching sandpipers and plovers scurry at the edge of the surf. As each wave receded, they pecked hurriedly and repeatedly at the sand before running from the wash of the next breaker. Curious, we searched the sand where they had been feeding, but could see nothing.

So intently were we looking that a breaker's last foaming reach caught us. As the water ebbed, I glanced down

Thimble-size periwinkle, an algae-eating snail, clings to a blade of cordgrass, submerged at high tide in a salt marsh. Cordgrass grows densely in salt marshes, providing food for scores of species. At low tide, a clapper rail seeking snails, crabs, and worms scurries through a Georgia marsh (opposite).

and saw a shell about the size of my fingernail. It immediately disappeared into the sand.

Quickly I grabbed up a large handful of sand and felt a slight stirring against my palm. When I rinsed away the sand, a tiny lavender-colored clam remained, its shells tightly closed. I recognized it as a coquina. These small bivalves live by the thousand in the tidal areas of sandy shores. To feed, they extend short tubular siphons and draw water into their bodies, filtering out microscopic nutrients. Coquinas, in turn, are an important source of food for many kinds of fishes and birds.

I set the coquina I was holding back down on the sand, and immediately a small pinkish foot extended from one end. In a series of swift jerks, the shell vanished beneath the surface. To accomplish this disappearing act, the coquina digs its foot into the sand, spreads it to act as an anchor, and then pulls itself down. The speed with which it happened— three or four movements a second—surprised me.

I was unprepared, as well, for the sheer number of coquinas, although the abundance of their empty shells should have given me a clue. Often, half a dozen appeared in a handful of sand.

Here, on a wave-swept beach of Cape Hatteras, I had discovered more hiding places.

I traveled slowly south from the Outer Banks, pausing to explore other salt marshes and sea islands on my way to Florida. There, I planned to dive in America's first underwater park, John Pennekamp Coral Reef State Park, just off Key Largo. In the company of veteran divers Doug and Laurie Cook, I jumped off a boat into another of the small realms of life just offshore. The clarity of the water in this shallow coral environment was surprising. I could see fish swimming more than 60 feet away.

The bottom was thick with coral and brightly hued fish. Some swam in solitary splendor, others in schools, like shifting streams of living color. Some were curious, even bold. A gray angelfish, just over a foot long, drifted to within inches of my face mask and peered in.

When I swam close to a clump of staghorn coral, a dusky damselfish about as big as my palm charged me, apparently defending its territory. It turned aside at the last minute, missing me by inches, then wheeled quickly to face me again. The pugnacious little fish seemed surprised that I had not retreated in terror, and again it charged. To put it at ease, I decided to move on.

Doug gestured me toward him, then leaned down and cupped his hand around a clump of green matter that looked like chewed celery. Surrounding it on the seafloor were pieces of white debris.

I thought these little round particles were simply sand. But Doug later explained that the plant we were examining was merman's shaving brush, (Continued on page 50)

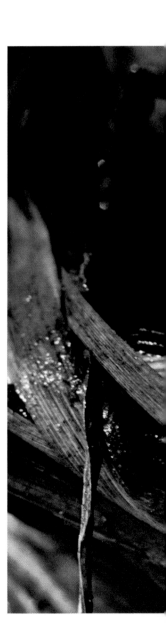

Eyestalks extended, a fierce-looking fiddler crab—just an inch across—clambers over cordgrass in a coastal salt marsh. Such marshes, nourished and cleansed by the tides, form one of the most organically productive areas in the world. The oozy mud, enriched by decaying material, becomes the basic source of nutrients in the marsh. Eventually, through a complex food web, it supports dozens of species. At low tide, land animals forage in marshes; during high tide, marine creatures swim in, finding shelter, food, and a place to breed. Because of the amount and diversity of life that salt marshes support, marine biologists call them nurseries of the sea. At top left, a two-inch-long sand shrimp eats emerald curtains of paper-thin sea lettuce, one of the

world's most widespread seaweeds. A small killifish (center, left) prowls a jungle of green algae. Half-buried in mud on a marsh floor, mussels use siphons to filter food from the water.

47

Spotting a school of menhaden, brown pelicans plunge headlong from 30 feet up into Atlantic waters off the coast of Georgia. Air sacs under a pelican's skin soften the impact of such dives, which take the bird two feet below the surface. Underwater (right), a pelican scoops a fish into its massive expandable pouch, beating a rival to the catch. Powerful jaws snap shut, and the bird surfaces. Before eating, the pelican bows its head to drain some three gallons of water from its pouch. Then, with an upward toss of its head, it swallows the fish. Pelicans eat an average of a pound of fish a day. Young pelicans learn to dive for food by imitating the techniques of adults. But many die of starvation in their first

year, possibly because they fail to master these skills. Strong fliers, brown pelicans have wingspans of as much as seven feet, but seldom stray far from shore. They nest in mangrove trees and hunt coastal waters. But, as man continues to encroach on wild wetlands, the pelican's habitat—and population—steadily declines. Already, the bird has nearly vanished in Louisiana and Texas. Scientists blame this disappearance, in part, on industrial and agricultural pollutants and chemicals in the water.

a kind of green alga that actually precipitates calcium compounds from seawater, and incorporates those minerals into its structure. I was especially interested in finding some of this alga—or a related species like the abundant *Halimeda*. I knew that much of the rock that underlies Florida is limestone derived in part from the remains of these simple plants. As I studied the flecks of calcium carbonate, I wondered if one day they, too, would be part of Florida.

A sudden movement caught my attention, and I watched as Laurie opened a plastic sandwich bag and pulled out chunks of frozen fish. She held a piece between her fingers, and an angelfish showed immediate interest. After a few moments of hesitation, the fish edged close enough to take a quick bite. I swam over to Laurie, took some of the bait, and also began tempting the angels. Soon, three were nibbling from my hand.

As they fed, I felt an urgent tap on my shoulder. I looked up to see that Laurie was pointing toward a four-foot-long barracuda. Its mouth brimming with jagged teeth, the fish cruised in lazy circles some ten feet above our heads. Laurie had no trouble making me understand that this was no creature to tempt with the bait.

A few minutes later, my air nearly gone, I swam toward the surface. As I rose, I glanced back at Laurie, who was still feeding the small fish. Suddenly a flash of silver whipped past me, aiming straight at her hand. I watched in horror as the barracuda snapped the bait from her fingers and streaked away. Startled, she dropped the bag of bait, jerked backward, and took several quick breaths, which produced a cloud of obscuring bubbles. When they cleared, I saw that Laurie was shakily holding up both hands to show Doug and me that she still had ten fingers.

She was lucky. Although barracudas generally keep their distance from divers, this bold one might have bitten her hand.

Near Padre Island, just off the coast of Texas, I learned of another potentially dangerous denizen of the shallow shores. Just as I started to wade into silty, foot-deep water, my companion, Dr. Lazern Sorensen, said, "You know, of course, that you have to slide your feet along as you wade so you don't step on the stingrays."

I stopped in midstride, my mind filled with visions of mammoth stingrays lurking on the bottom, armed with poisonous barbs, and waiting for prey. Dr. Sorensen must have seen my expression, for he hastened to reassure me. "In shallow waters like this, there will just be young ones not more than a foot across, and they'll try to avoid you. But even the sting of a small one can be painful. Today, the water is turbid—they can't see you coming, and you can't see them. So it's best to slide your feet and nudge them to avoid stepping on one." I heeded his advice and very, very carefully slid my feet along the muddy bottom.

We waded through the vast beds of sea grasses that

Edge of the shallow shores, a shelf fringing the island of San Salvador in the Bahamas plummets from azure shallows to inky depths. Divers (opposite) descend the vertical wall of the coral reef, studying life forms along the drop-off.

50

carpet the shallow waters of Laguna Madre between Padre Island and the Texas coast. Dr. Sorensen, Director of Pan American University's Marine Biology Laboratory in the town of South Padre Island, has studied the ecology of the island and its waters for some 20 years. This day, he carried a bucket and a fine-meshed dip net as we shuffled into the water. A few yards offshore, he swept the net in several wide arcs, then deftly flipped the contents into an inch or two of water in the bottom of the bucket. I peered in.

The water was alive with wriggling, frantically jerking organisms. Dr. Sorensen reached into the bucket, cupped a palmful of water, and held it up for my inspection. I quickly recognized the animals: shrimp. More than a score of the crustaceans, each but a fraction of an inch long, stirred the water in his hand.

Dr. Sorensen explained that during this youthful stage in their existence, shrimp congregate by the million in these coastal waters. Later, as the crustaceans mature, they migrate from the safety of the grassy areas to the open sea. "Such beds of sea grass flourish along warm shores throughout the world," he said. "They're not just nurseries for shrimp, though; dozens of ocean creatures use these areas as havens during their early development.

"To get a true feel for the wealth of life here," he continued, "you should put on a face mask and snorkel and take a close look at the grassy beds underwater." That afternoon, I took Dr. Sorensen's advice.

As I lay floating facedown in knee-deep water that afternoon, I recalled some of the diverse creatures that Dr. Sorensen had caught in his net: tiny pipefish, slender as a toothpick; miniature crabs; fish a minnow would dwarf. But as quiet as I remained, I could see no animals in the silt-laden water.

I shifted my attention to the sea grass, waving serenely in a slight current. Each blade was filmy, covered with algae that looked like tiny leaves on a twig. I uprooted a few strands of grass and lifted them from the water. In the air, the algae immediately collapsed into a brownish scum that covered the narrow blade. Again I peered into the water. There, each filament of algae was supported and extended, brushed gently by the tide.

Later, when I returned to the marine laboratory, I told Dr. Sorensen that I was amazed at the denseness of the sea grass. Nodding, he asked me how many animals I had seen. Somewhat disappointed, I replied, "Only a few mullet, and those at quite a distance."

He smiled. "Those grass beds make pretty good hiding places, don't they?"

I left Texas and the shallows fringing the coast of the United States eager to explore a drop-off, where the relatively shallow ocean bottom bordering the land plunges to the deep sea. It is a vibrantly rich zone with a multitude of life forms, from small fish and crustaceans that hug the coastline to large predators of the open ocean.

I was fortunate. Sylvia Earle, author of the introduction to this book, and photographer Al Giddings were planning a trip to such a drop-off in the Bahamas, and they invited me to join them.

Within a few hours of our arrival on the island of San Salvador, we were off on a dive. The water was clear and the color breathtaking—vivid sponges grew in patches of bright orange, deep rust, and fluorescent yellow. A group of blue parrotfish fed head down. They grazed the stony surface of the coral, spitting out bits of hard exterior skeleton and devouring the algae growing there.

Cruising among the smaller fishes—and ignoring them with regal dignity—was a large Nassau grouper. Its eyes, I was startled to find, moved independently of each other. I extended my gloved hand, wiggling my fingers as I had seen other divers do. The grouper, more than two feet long, edged closer, coming within inches before it retreated in apparent disappointment at not being fed. As I swam off, it tagged along, like a puppy that was trying to be affectionate without getting in the way.

I glanced to my right and saw Sylvia indicating that I should follow her. For a few moments, I glided slowly just a few feet above the coral reef we had been exploring. Then, suddenly, unexpectedly, the bottom dropped away. I felt as if I had stepped from the top floor of a skyscraper and was simply hanging in the air without falling. The coral plunged abruptly into an abyss of deepening blue. Sylvia had beckoned me, it seemed, to the edge of the world.

In fact, I had come to the very rim of the shallow shores. Beyond this point existed open seas and deeps. The sheerness of the drop surprised me—I had anticipated a more gradual decline—and for several days I explored the upper extent of the drop-off. One morning, though, as we loaded our gear aboard the boat, Al Giddings suggested that we make a deeper dive.

To conserve our air supply, we descended quickly, dropping down the vertical wall of the reef. Much of it was dense with algae, particularly *Caulerpa*, a green alga found throughout tropical waters.

The needle of my depth gauge finally stopped at 200 feet, the deepest I had ever been. Al pointed out a clump of feathery black coral. I anchored myself to this eerie-looking growth, then glanced up.

Far above, the top of the reef was a dark edge of shadow across the brightness of the shimmering surface. I felt as if I were at the bottom of a deep well—until I looked below me. The blue gradually faded into infinite blackness that had no dimension, no up, no down. For a brief moment, I felt an overwhelming impulse to push off from the coral and explore the mysteries that lay hidden there. It was unknown, alluring, beautiful. Then Sylvia appeared, interrupting my

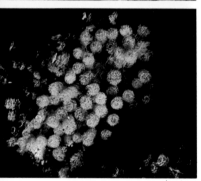

Feathery red alga (upper), one of hundreds of species in tropical waters, brightens the underwater wilds off San Salvador. Along with the green alga (lower), it thrives at depths of more than a hundred feet. Near the Equator, clear water and the direct rays of the sun allow plant life to live at depths of several hundred feet.

52

thoughts. She motioned me upward. It was time to leave—ten minutes had passed quickly.

As it was, even that short time proved to be almost too long, for I ran out of air on the way up. I had been swimming steadily upward, examining the reef wall, reflecting on what I had seen. I was about ten yards from the standby air hoses where we would allow our bodies to decompress—void from our blood and tissues the nitrogen that gathers at depth—when the air cut out. I sucked hard on my mouthpiece, but got nothing. Grisly stories about the bends—the crippling sickness caused by nitrogen bubbles forming in the bloodstream of a diver who surfaces too quickly without a decompression stop—flashed through my mind. I kicked hard toward the hoses. My lungs began to ache, and then to burn. Just when I thought I could swim no farther, I reached an air hose, jammed it to my mouth, and pulled in the freshest, most satisfying breath I have ever taken.

On San Salvador, I made not only my deepest dive but also one of my shallowest. One afternoon I traveled to the southern end of the island to investigate the mangrove tangles of Pigeon Creek. Forests of mangrove trees flourish in such protected, shallow areas that are inundated by both salt and fresh water. The trees themselves grow in the water, their support roots intermingling in great arching tangles. The labyrinth of trunks and roots below the surface nurtures a system of life that rivals the salt marsh in its diversity and richness.

I spent a fascinating afternoon poking among the mangroves of Pigeon Creek and discovering some of the residents there. On a single ten-inch-long stalk of half-decayed turtle grass, I counted 21 miniature hermit crabs, all jockeying for the choicest bits of algae. With their borrowed shells on their backs, they looked like so many backpackers.

I watched a small barracuda, just eight inches long, as it cruised among the mangroves alone and seemingly fearless. In this world of miniature fish, it was king. It circled me several times, eying me with the same curious yet wary expression of its larger brothers. At another point I observed young parrotfish nibbling on mangrove leaves, which provide nourishment here much as do the grasses in a salt marsh. But it still surprised me to find fish eating green leaves off the branches of trees.

On a rainswept morning several days later, Sylvia, Al, and I headed north under a bank of gray clouds that soon drifted apart, leaving an azure sky in their wake. We were hoping to find a spotted dolphin so well known to the islanders that they have named him Sandy. Marine mammals, spotted dolphins generally are creatures of the open sea, but they may visit the shallow shores to frolic. Sandy, a male about three years old, apparently lives permanently near San Salvador, swimming playfully with snorkelers and scuba divers when they come to visit. As we approached the

Mermaid's wineglass (upper) and Halimeda *draw calcium compounds from the sea. These minerals form skeletonlike deposits that remain when the algae die.*

53

M. TIMOTHY O'KEEFE (LOWER, LEFT); OTHERS BY AL GIDDINGS, SEA FILMS, INC.

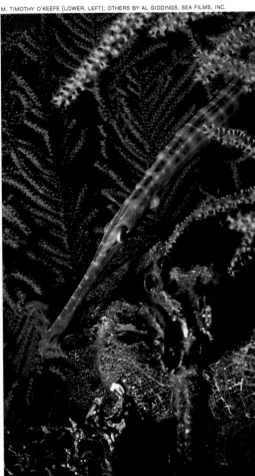

Collecting algae samples in a mesh bag, Sylvia Earle skims past an undersea meadow of turtle grass in Pigeon Creek, San Salvador. "It was a great sensation," she said, "to glide through that grass and feel it brushing against me." A spiny lobster (left) rests on the bottom near a rock crevice. "I came face to face with that lobster, and he held his ground," said Sylvia. "He seemed as interested in me as I was in him." During the day, spiny lobsters usually stay hidden in their homes. A trumpetfish (above, right) hovers in a forest of flexible coral and green algae 50 feet down. Protective coloration allows the trumpetfish, which can reach three feet in length, to hang unnoticed. When a fish swims by, the predator strikes so swiftly that the fish seems to disappear. At far left, an Atlantic bay scallop, two inches in diameter, keeps watch with blue eyes in the shallows off Florida. These scallops have as many as 100 eyes, but they detect only changes in light.

area where Sandy had last been sighted, the dolphin suddenly appeared, splashing a welcome in towering leaps.

I immediately put on my diving gear and followed the others into the water. When I reached the bottom about 30 feet down, I saw that Sylvia was already cavorting with Sandy. She had one arm around his body, and was scratching him just behind the flippers. Sandy rolled upside down and paused for a moment, then swam a few yards off. When he returned, Sylvia slowly moved away and Sandy followed, the short, arching strokes of his tail gracefully duplicating Sylvia's kicks.

Soon, Sandy headed to the surface to breathe. A moment later, I felt a gentle nudge against my leg. Sandy was waiting for attention. I stroked his sleek gray side, smooth and silken to the touch. As Sandy rolled over, I noticed a thin trickle of blood seeping from a small cut in the corner of his mouth. Sylvia later told me that the wound might have been inflicted by the beak of a cuttlefish or a squid, ingredients of a dolphin's diet.

For more than half an hour Sandy played with us, moving from one diver to another. I was spellbound; Sandy's affection and playfulness reminded me of Banco, my own Great Dane. For the first time in my life, I tried to talk to an undersea creature. However, because my mouth was filled with breathing apparatus, all I could manage were grunts and groans. But Sandy seemed to understand that I was attempting to communicate, and peered intently at me as I made my noises.

My air supply soon began to run low, and I turned back toward the boat. Within seconds, Sandy appeared beside me. I grabbed the dolphin just behind his front flippers, and he began towing me up. Near the boat I let go, patted Sandy one last time, and bid a quiet farewell to this friendly, intelligent animal.

In central Florida, I encountered another marine mammal—the manatee. Weighing as much as a ton, these ponderous creatures live in rivers, in estuaries, and along the shorelines of warm coasts. They are gentle, shy beasts—often called sea cows—that drift in shallows while browsing on water plants.

I joined Buddy Powell of the U. S. Fish and Wildlife Service in Crystal River, Florida, to search for manatees. Hardly a breeze rippled the still surface of Kings Bay as we anchored Buddy's houseboat *Trichechus*—named for the genus to which manatees belong—under a gray and threatening December sky.

We climbed to the roof to scan the waters around us for signs of the lumbering giants. After several minutes, Buddy called out, "There's one—no, two. A female and her calf." I could barely discern a faint outline of massive brown, shaped like an inflated ten-foot cigar, with another, smaller shape beside it.

I had just focused on this pair when Buddy wheeled

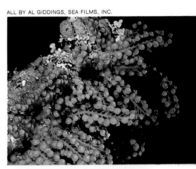

Caulerpa *sprouts from the wall of a coral reef off San Salvador. Sylvia Earle picks some of the alga, which has spherical green blades (upper). Author Bob Morrison samples a sprig of the plant, reporting, "It tastes just like fresh lettuce."*

Inquisitive Nassau grouper, hoping for a snack, approaches author Morrison above a reef near San Salvador. The two-foot-long fish, which weighs eight pounds, can quickly change color to camouflage itself from larger predators. Above, the grouper permits small gobies to clean irritating parasites from its head and gills. These gobies—and several other species of fishes and crustaceans— develop symbiotic relationships with larger creatures, feeding on the damaging parasites.

and pointed in the opposite direction. "There should be one over there. Yes! See it?"

"How did you know that one was there?" I asked in amazement as I spotted the manatee he indicated. "You were looking in the opposite direction."

"I heard it," he explained. "Every few minutes manatees stick their valved nostrils above the surface to take a breath. That inhalation is what you have to listen for." I concentrated on listening.

Soon, a manatee surfaced, its whiskered nose protruding above the water just a couple of dozen yards away. I heard it breathe. The sound was like a deep sigh, and it lasted for two or three seconds. With Buddy's help I quickly counted about 15 of the creatures swimming and feeding in Kings Bay. Colder weather was beginning to set in, and they had moved from the cooler waters of the Gulf of Mexico to the Crystal River, which is fed by springs issuing water at a steady 74° F.

To find out more about these mammals, I talked with Blair Irvine, a biologist with the Fish and Wildlife Service. "There is still a lot we don't know about manatees," he told me. "We're not sure how many exist along the Florida coasts, or exactly where they go in the warmer months when they leave such protected refuges as Crystal River. We don't know how long they live. Because the animals are so shy, they're difficult to study."

After spending a few hours snorkeling in Crystal River, I understood better just how shy the animals are. By moving slowly and quietly through the water, I managed to get close enough to one animal to watch it cropping *Hydrilla*, a flowering freshwater plant.

After a moment, the manatee saw me and moved off, still munching, with stems of the plant streaming from its mouth. I could see the half-moon toenails on its blunt front flippers, and was reminded that Irvine had told me that manatees are distantly related to elephants.

During most of my afternoon snorkeling, I saw little more than the backs of manatees. Most of them bore scars from motorboat propellers; careless boatmen are the major enemies of this bulky mammal. But one did turn toward me, briefly regarding me with black button eyes. It had an expression of perpetual contentment. Then, using only its tail for propulsion, it swam away, its motion surprisingly graceful and fluid considering its bulk.

As I watched it disappear slowly from sight, I reflected on the many zones of life that I had discovered as I explored the shallow shores. I had learned to appreciate the minuscule as well as the mighty, to uncover the beauty in a muddy marsh or a sluggish stream, to find a complex web of life where at first I thought no creatures existed.

Never again would a seashore, a salt marsh, a mangrove swamp seem deserted to me. I had learned to search out the hiding places.

THE

Surging waves lash craggy sea stacks off the coast of Washington. Such cold, nutrient-rich waters as these harbor abundant life—from tiny hermit crabs to graceful sea mammals.

ROCKY COASTS

By Linda McCarter Bridge

Shafts of light from a dawning sun edged between the peaks of the Santa Lucia mountains. The growing warmth soon began to burn away the mist veiling the California coast. From a rocky, surf-battered ledge, I watched a furry brown sea otter begin to stir.

It tossed aside strands of seaweed that it had used to moor itself while resting, and quickly disappeared below the surface. Just as quickly it returned, clutching a spiny red sea urchin under its left foreleg and a flat rock under its right. Floating on its back and using its chest as a table, the sea otter pounded the urchin's shell against the rock. Then it scraped out the urchin's thick orange roe with long shovel-like teeth.

Sleek, streamlined, and insulated with thick fur, the sea otter is well adapted to life in the cold, rocky realm it inhabits. Such rugged coastlines, which stretch along the entire western coast of the United States and Canada, harbor a rich variety of plant and animal life. Barnacles, mussels, and abalones cling to the rocks; surfperch and rockfish glide among swaying strands of kelp; eels, octopuses, and lobsters hide in dark holes on the bottom.

A similar world—filled with different species—runs from Labrador to Massachusetts on the Atlantic coast. In both areas, and in many like regions around the world, the shoreline is washed by cold seas that range in temperature from 45° to 55° F. These seas are continuously replenished with nutrients stirred from the bottom.

As I watched the otter dive again to that bountiful seafloor, I wondered what this coast was like centuries ago when otters were abundant here. Once they had populated the shores of the northern Pacific from Japan to Alaska to lower California—a 6,000-mile-long rim of rugged coastline lashed by wind and wave. In the 1700's fur hunters from many countries began to pursue the sea otter for its pelt, which commanded a high price. Otters were hunted almost to extinction before an international treaty, enacted in 1911, protected the animal.

Surviving otter colonies slowly began to multiply. Today, some 120,000 otters live along Alaska's shores, and California's central coast supports a growing population of about 2,000. Jack Ames, a marine biologist with California's Department of Fish and Game, keeps track of the otters' expanding range, which now extends for 180 miles between Santa Cruz and Avila Beach.

In his Monterey office, Jack handed me an otter pelt, the thickest, most luxuriant fur I've ever touched. "Sea otters don't have blubber like other marine mammals," he explained. "They rely on two things to keep them warm—air trapped in their fur and a high metabolic rate. To fuel its metabolic furnace, an otter eats about ten pounds of food a day. In a year, the otters that live along the California coast can devour as much as eight million pounds. That's why this coast will change somewhat as otters return to their former range. Because of their voracious appetites, they drastically affect many species they prey on."

I asked Jack what otters eat. He laughed and said, "What *don't* they eat? Otters are opportunistic feeders. Although they prefer abalones and sea urchins, they'll also eat crabs, clams, snails, mussels, scallops, chitons, barnacles, squids, octopuses, and occasionally fish. They'll even chew the rays off sea stars—a creature that hardly anything else will touch. Once I saw an otter bring up a pop-top can and bite it open. Then he pulled out and gobbled up a small octopus that was hiding inside. Within 15 minutes, he had found seven more cans and five octopuses."

A few days later, I drifted in a boat through mustard-colored kelp in Monterey Bay, hoping to locate more otters. I spotted one young female resting in a bed of seaweed, her shiny brown eyes blinking in the sunlight. She stretched, sneezed, dived, and soon surfaced a few feet from the boat, crunching on a small kelp crab. When she finished, she surprised me by pulling out pieces of surfgrass and kelp that she had tucked under a foreleg. She used them like dental floss and toothpicks.

Watching such antics of sea otters quickly fills a morning. They cavort and frolic almost endlessly, it seems. But these smallest of marine mammals are much more than marine clowns. They seem to have such an impact on the ecology of the cold shores, in fact, that some marine biologists call them a keystone species. By eating sea urchins—one of their favorite foods—they help maintain the balance of life in the extensive kelp forests off the coast of California. The purple sea urchin, whose population dramatically increased during the period when the sea otter was overhunted, feeds on the kelp plant. Acres of thick kelp forests, which provide habitats for millions of animals, were reduced to marine deserts by a combination of these urchins and the increasing pollution from coastal development.

Many marine biologists believe that the return of the otter will help save these productive ecosystems. Along Alaska's coast, in areas where otters have reduced sea urchin populations, kelp beds have again flourished, providing shelter and nutrients for more marine life.

For years, all I knew of kelp was that it washed up onto the beach in smelly, decaying piles. When I learned that kelp grows into vast submarine forests that harbor countless exotic and beautiful creatures, I decided to investigate firsthand. With diver-photographer Lewis Trusty, I sailed to Santa Catalina Island, home of the University of Southern California's Marine Science Center. Tucked into Big Fisherman's Cove and bounded by high rocky cliffs, the center is sheltered from most prevailing winds.

I sought out Bob Given, director of the center, to learn more about kelp. "Kelp forests," Bob said, "are to rocky coasts as coral reefs are to tropical waters. Both are important ecosystems that support a wide range of species. But a

DOUG M. WILSON

Scavenger of the Northwest coast, a glaucous-winged gull plucks a clam from a tidal flat in Washington's Puget Sound. The gull cracked open the clam's shell by dropping it on a hard surface from the air. When the tide ebbs in such rocky regions, pools of seawater preserve marine life until the high tide washes back in.

coral reef is alive only at the top, whereas a kelp forest is three-dimensional—life abounds at the top, in the middle, and at the bottom."

Like Jack's beanstalk, giant kelp is one of the fastest growing plants in the world, Bob explained. A frond of this species can grow more than a foot a day and may reach lengths of 200 feet. The frond has a slender stipe, or stalk, that sprouts long, wrinkled blades—each supported by an air-filled bladder. This enormous plant, like all seaweeds, does not have true roots. A clump of rootlike tentacles called a holdfast anchors the kelp to rocks on the bottom. Dozens of separate fronds grow from each holdfast and, buoyed by the bladders, rise to the surface where they form a thick interwoven canopy. The blades in this canopy receive the sunlight necessary for photosynthesis. The nutrients produced are transferred back down the stipe to the holdfast.

Later that afternoon, I joined Lew Trusty on an exploratory trip into a kelp forest. Equipped with face masks, snorkels, and fins, we swam to Blue Cavern Point, where I found a world of riotous color. Sponges in scarlet, yellow, purple, and orange blanketed the rocks. Small red tube worms waved their plumes as they fed on passing plankton. Green and red algae billowed in the surge. A school of young blacksmith fish, garbed in orange and blue, darted around us. Then, suddenly, I was nose to nose with a garibaldi. We peered at each other for several seconds before it swam away. I watched this little red-orange fish maneuver gracefully in that dense kelp jungle. I had to worry constantly about becoming entangled.

Lew tugged at my arm and pointed. Just a few feet below us, four moray eels darted into and out of crevices in the rock. Their big mouths repeatedly gaped open, exposing needle-sharp teeth. "That's not a threat display," he explained later. "They open their mouths to get water to their gills. I don't think the eels here are really that aggressive, but I certainly wouldn't want to find out by reaching into one of their rock crevices, either."

That evening for dinner, Lew and I joined Jim Coyer and Jack Engle, young marine biologists who were working at the Marine Center. I mentioned that we had seen moray eels and garibaldis that day. Jack recalled an experience he once had when he was offering food to a moray eel. "I had just pulled out a big chunk of bait," he said, "when a little garibaldi zoomed up out of nowhere, drove this ferocious-looking eel back into its hole, and grabbed the food. I was amazed at how aggressive it was."

"Those garibaldis are highly territorial, too," Lew added. "I've had them bite my cameras, my face mask, and my gloves while trying to drive me away as I was filming their nests." He explained that the male prepares the nest by cleaning a rock of most large plant life. Then he allows specific kinds of small red algae to grow back. After a female lays her eggs on the algae, the male chases her off and fiercely protects the egg mass until the young hatch.

"Actually," said Jim, "that's not unusual behavior. Many rocky-coast fish have similar life-styles." To study the interactions among fishes, invertebrates, and kelp, Jim has made nearly a thousand dives in kelp forests, and gradually has been able to define the complex food web there. "Incredible numbers of animals—ranging from insects to mammals—depend on the kelp," he said. "It provides surface area for small animals to inhabit. Fish feed on these creatures, and sea lions and seals eat the fish."

Next morning, diving in a kelp forest in Fourth of July

Cove, a narrow inlet on the north shore of Santa Catalina Island, I felt as if I were entering a huge, undulating mansion of infinite rooms. The ceiling of this grand house was the thick canopy drifting on the surface; the walls were the plants' tangled stipes. Halls and passageways among the kelp plants seemed to lead to different rooms, which often had lacy curtains of blades. The inhabitants of this mansion were the colorful creatures that glided among the rooms.

Gold-colored kelp snails with gray shells and magenta nudibranchs with orange gills crept along the billowing fronds. Pink barnacles encrusted the blades, and yellow kelp crabs scurried past them. Purple sea urchins and red sea cucumbers moved slowly along the bottom on their tube feet. Sea stars in reds and blues inched past sea anemones in greens and tangerines.

Lew slashed open a sea urchin *(Continued on page 70)*

Eyes bulging, arrow squids hover above their egg cases in a submarine canyon off California. Large schools of squids leave the open sea to spawn in these waters, anchoring the seven-inch-long egg cases to rocks or seaweed. Each case contains several hundred eggs, and sometimes the cases blanket half a square mile of seafloor.

(Continued on page 70)

65

*Striped eyes of a hermit
crab peer from beneath a
wavy top shell. Bright
algae encrusts the shell and
the crab's rocky perch off
southern California.
Lacking stomach armor,
the two-inch-long crab
carries the empty shell for
protection and as a home,
using two tail hooks to hold
it in place. Crusher claws
fit together to block the
entrance when the crab
retreats inside. As it
grows, the hermit crab
moves into larger shells,
sometimes dislodging
another crab. Hermit crabs
live in tidal pools and down
to depths of more than a
hundred feet. They eat
any available animal
matter—dead or alive.*

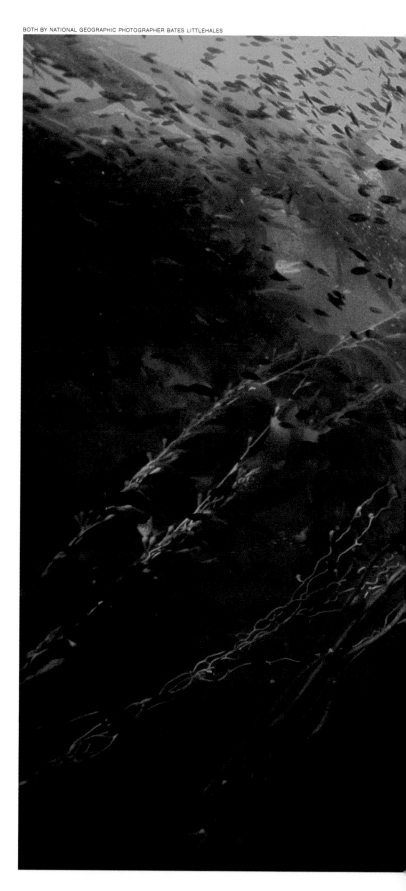

Lush submarine forest of giant kelp near Baja California nurtures animal life as abundant and diverse as that in a terrestrial forest. Hundreds of blacksmith fish surround a diver swimming past a column of kelp, a kind of seaweed that reaches dozens of feet from the seafloor to the surface. Below, a giant kelpfish glides past a meandering stipe, or stalk, of the kelp plant. Giant kelp flourishes in cold coastal areas around the world, sometimes growing more than a foot a day.

with his knife, and suddenly we were surrounded by hungry sheepsheads, gobies, and garibaldis. A latecomer, a crevice kelpfish that had been camouflaged among rocks and algae, slipped in to steal the last morsel.

From the kelp forests of Santa Catalina Island, Lew and I sailed 32 miles to Santa Barbara Island to meet another of the rocky coast's characters. Stars still lit the sky as I crept toward dark shapes piled in heaps on the rocky ledges. Soon the sun rose, and with it came a deafening amount of noise—deep yawns, belches, and loud barks.

A rookery of some two thousand California sea lions was stirring, the animals beginning another day of fishing and playing. Stocky but streamlined, these mammals look awkward on land. Large males can weigh 600 pounds and measure some eight feet long. During mating season, a big bull often has a harem of a dozen or more females. Bulls spend most of their time patrolling their harems and battling potential suitors—the young bachelors of the rookery.

Raising clouds of dust, the sea lions lumbered down to the water and dived in. Within two hours, most of the rookery's stragglers were swimming, although some shifted about on their flippers like reluctant children before taking that first plunge.

I envied the sea lion's ability to live both in the sea and on the shore as I later struggled into my diving gear. When I submerged, the sea was alive with sleek torpedo-shaped sea lions, their brown fur appearing gray in the underwater light. Darting among kelp fronds, they twisted, pivoted, and looped in a graceful display of acrobatics. They are as swift and agile in the sea as they are clumsy on land.

The sea lions zipped along the surface and plunged to depths of 30 feet or more. With these playful mammals as companions, I began exploring their world. When I reached the bottom, I came upon a creature that I had never seen before in the wild—an abalone. A type of marine snail, an abalone carries a rough, flattened, oval-shaped shell that is lined inside with rainbow-hued mother-of-pearl. An abalone moves along the bottom with a big muscular foot, eating algae and kelp with a rasplike tongue. At the slightest hint of danger, it uses that foot to clamp to a rock with a force that can equal 400 pounds.

Because of their tasty meat, abalones are called the "sirloin of the sea," and they have been fished extensively for decades. This fishing, combined with the growing numbers of sea otters and their taste for abalones, has reduced the population in many areas. One answer to man's demand for abalones is to raise them commercially. But this industry, I learned, is only in the formative stages.

Near Estero Bay, 175 miles north of Los Angeles, I talked with Frank Oakes, a thoughtful young marine biologist who runs the hatching end of a fledgling commercial abalone fishery. Frank took me into the spawning room where fiberglass buckets hold millions of microscopic abalones. "First of all," he explained, "it's difficult to get them to spawn. Once they do, and the young are hatched, that first week of life is extremely critical. Conditions have to be just right: temperature, water circulation, and the amount of light and food. Though a mature female abalone produces more than two million eggs each year, the mortality rate is unbelievably high. It probably is in the wild, too—survival is tough in the sea.

"Our goal," he continued, "is to raise about two million abalones a year. To protect them from otters and other predators, we'll put them in cages down in the sea until they mature. Then we'll harvest them. It may seem strange raising abalones—wild creatures—this way. But the original balance of life along this coast is gone forever. The return of the sea otter helps restore it some, but you can never really turn back the clock. Man is part of the equation now, and we have to accept that and adjust to it."

Several weeks later, I saw a natural abalone nursery off a lonely stretch of Mexico's Baja California. The beach was rugged. Steep cliffs soared into desert hills, and offshore islets and pinnacles rose from azure seas. The deep fissures, overhangs, and holes of these eroded lava rocks provide perfect homes for abalones. In one rocky crevice, tiny abalones—some as small as pinheads—hugged the rock walls in countless numbers. Along the bottom, I found a few mature abalones, each about seven inches across.

At dusk that evening, just as the sun painted the sky a saffron color, a lone fisherman came over to my camping spot and offered some abalones he had gathered. Then, out of a burlap sack, he pulled a spiny lobster to complement the abalone dinner. To me, the 15-inch-long crustacean, studded with appendages, spines, and long antennae, looked like a giant insect. Spiny lobsters are related to New England lobsters but lack the large claws.

The complicated life cycle of the California spiny lobster is being investigated by marine biologist Jack Engle at the Marine Science Center on Santa Catalina Island. Jack, a robust, enthusiastic man, finds the camouflaged young of the spiny lobster—each no more than four inches long—simply by seeing an irregularity on the seafloor. He captures them not with traps or nets but with his bare hands.

"Spiny lobsters drift as tiny transparent plankton in the ocean for a year," Jack told me. "Then, usually in mid-August, the larvae settle into a surfgrass nursery. They hide during the day and forage at night. They eat mollusks, which they can easily break open with their jaws. As the lobsters grow toward maturity, they shed their shells about a dozen times.

"By the next summer," Jack continued, "they begin to mix with adult lobsters that migrate into the shallow grassy areas. Then in early fall, the juveniles leave the nursery and follow the adults out into deeper water. A new generation of

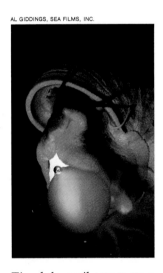

Tiny kelp snail grazes on a gas-filled float, one of dozens of bladders that buoy kelp blades. These blades absorb the sun's energy and produce nutrients for the entire seaweed. Torn loose in a storm, a kelp holdfast (opposite)—the rootlike structure that anchors the plant to the bottom—drifts toward the surface. Most such uprooted plants soon wash ashore and die. Dense kelp forests provide a multistoried home for scores of animal species—crabs and worms on the bottom, snails and sea slugs on the blades, and fishes throughout.

71

Clutching a red sea urchin in its forepaws, a sea otter spurts to the surface in Monterey Bay, California. At right, another otter uses his chest for a table as he eats the flesh of a sea urchin. The otter broke open the urchin's shell by pounding it against a rock on his chest. Otters help control the numbers of sea urchins, which can devastate kelp forests by undermining the plants' holdfasts. Inch-wide white urchins (bottom, right) graze on a blade of kelp. Abalones (center), another favorite food of the otter, cling to rocks on the seafloor. In one day, an otter can devour 12 abalones, 20 sea urchins, 11 rock crabs, 60 kelp crabs, and 112 snails—some ten pounds of food.

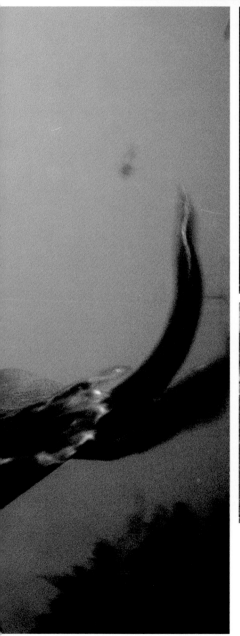

larval lobsters soon settles into the surfgrass, and the cycle begins again."

On the East Coast, such cycles and migrations are important to thousands of fishermen who seek the delectable New England lobster, *Homarus americanus*, on rocky ocean bottoms from New York to Labrador.

Recent research indicates that there may be two distinct lobster populations off the coast of New England: an inshore group that stays near the coast, and an offshore group that migrates each spring to shallow water. These lobsters may cover several hundred miles each year, walking as much as six miles a day. Apparently, most are females coming to warmer waters to spawn.

"Migration is a confusing subject to most of us," said Wendell Seavey, a 35-year-old lobsterman who lives in Bass Harbor on Mount Desert Island, Maine. "Lobstermen have always thought that there's just one group that migrates in the winter from shallow waters to deeper waters because they are calmer and warmer. Now, marine biologists tell us that there may be two populations. Whatever the case, we still have to haul twice as deep in the winter to find lobsters."

Wendell, like many other people, wonders if lobsters are being caught faster than they can reproduce. "The catch is way down now," he said, "but I'm sure it will change with time. In this business, you have to take it like nature gives it to you."

Whether or not the lobster population is declining, heavy fishing of the crustaceans seems to be causing a gradual shift in the ecological balance along the coasts of New England and the Maritime Provinces of Canada. Marine biologists are discovering large bare areas in once-lush kelp beds, with droves of sea urchins nearby. One of the urchin's most effective natural predators is the lobster.

I was struck by the surprising analogy between eastern and western coasts. In both of the areas, man overconsumed major predators: lobsters and sea otters. Their prey, two different species of sea urchins, rapidly multiplied in number. The sea urchins then overgrazed the kelp forests, destroying an important habitat for dozens of species of fish and other marine animals.

"It's a potentially grim situation," said David Mills. "If the lobsters are disappearing, it's bad for the fishermen, but it's disastrous for coastal marine life." I spent an evening with David and Audrey Mills touring their imaginative, homemade, "please touch" oceanarium, which is housed in an old hardware store in the town of Southwest Harbor on Mount Desert Island.

Self-taught naturalists, they display the spectrum of life found in Maine's coastal waters. Most of the specimens are caught in the nets of local fishermen. In fact, as I examined David's tanks, a smiling lobsterman came in holding a large lobster. Its shell looked like a lacquered autumn leaf with splotches of orange, gold, and *(Continued on page 80)*

FLIP NICKLIN, SCIENCE APPLICATION, INC. (OPPOSITE); OTHERS BY NEIL G. MCDANIEL, OCEAN IMAGES

Spindly-legged cleaner shrimp pick parasites from a moray eel in its rocky lair off Baja California (opposite). Powerful jaws of a wolf-eel (above) crush a sea urchin bristling with spines. Another wolf-eel eyes a sea urchin. These six-foot-long eels live off California and British Columbia.

DAVID LAUR (ABOVE); NEIL G. MCDANIEL, OCEAN IMAGES

Resembling an interstellar spaceship, a brightly colored nudibranch, or sea slug, extends pointed gills as it glides through cold waters. The two-inch-long creature, which inhabits kelp forests and other regions of dense vegetation, breathes through these protruding gills. Mollusks without shells, nudibranchs feed on sea anemones, hydroid polyps, and sponges.

Clustered on a rock 66 feet down in Jervis Inlet, British Columbia, sea anemones wave sinuous tentacles that entice prey. Poisonous barbs line the inches-long tentacles of these animals. Of sea anemones, famed author John Steinbeck once wrote that they seem to "expand like soft and brilliant flowers, inviting any tired and perplexed animal to lie for a moment in their arms." As the animal moves into reach, "the stinging arms shoot tiny narcotic needles into the prey and it grows weak and perhaps sleepy while the searing caustic digestive acids melt its body down."

Armored gladiators, American lobsters (below) fight for territory on a ledge crowded with urchins and mussels. With its large pincer, one lobster clubs the other. In such battles, the foot-long crustaceans usually only joust, but occasionally they will fight to the death. Solitary animals, lobsters guard small defined areas from Labrador to the Carolinas, normally at depths from 20 to 1,500 feet.

Mottled lobster steals bait from a lobster trap (upper) using its extendable mouth parts. Lobsters wield their pincers—one a crusher with bumpy molarlike teeth, the other a ripper with sharp spiny teeth—to fight and feel. If a lobster loses one of these claws, it eventually grows a new one. Weak eyes detect only motion, so the lobster must rely on other senses to hunt. Microscopic hairs cover its body—as many as a hundred thousand on the claws and legs alone. These hairs transmit impulses to the central nervous system as the lobster feels in holes and crevices with its appendages. Hairs on the long antennae and mouth, sensitive to chemical changes, help the lobster detect smells. Above, two lobsters attempt to mate, but in vain. Mating can occur only after the female has molted. She protects her life in this vulnerable state by emitting a scent that not only attracts the male but also discourages him from making her his next meal.

yellow. "I'd rather you show her off here," he told David, "than me eat her for dinner."

David put the lobster in a tank with many others. Nearby were several empty shells abandoned by lobsters as they grew larger. I asked David how lobsters get out of their shells. "They respond to a physiological trigger and begin to shrink," he explained. "At the same time, their shells begin to dissolve in two places. The shoulders become soft so the claws can pass through. A line on the back also softens and the shell hinges up there, permitting the lobster to escape. It's like backing out of a jumpsuit through a waistline slit."

After pulling its body through the narrow opening, a lobster must extract its 38 appendages—each specially adapted to feel, bite, fight, grasp, walk, or swim. The lobster is truly an engineering marvel of hinged, jointed, and feathery parts.

But it has a rival in its cousin the barnacle, a resident of all rocky coasts. Like other crustaceans, barnacles are free swimmers during the larval stages. When they reach shallow water, they use sensitive antennae to select a spot—usually a rock or shell—to settle down permanently. They cement themselves to this spot headfirst, then secrete a limy fortress. Inside, four movable plates can close, retaining water when the tide ebbs and thus protecting the animal.

Carrying a magnifying glass, I went barnacle hunting along the jumbled glacier-carved shores of Maine's Acadia National Park. The fractured granite cliffs were brushed by a wispy fog and fringed by forests—bright autumn leaves stood out sharply against the deep green of conifers. It was low tide, and I found clusters of barnacles drying in the sun, their volcano-shaped shells pinched shut. In nearby tidal pools—small depressions in the rock that still held water—the barnacles remained open. Through my magnifying glass, I watched a barnacle sweep its feathery legs through the water, kicking minute bits of food toward its mouth.

I became mesmerized by the gentle rhythm of the barnacle, and thought how, when open, it looked like a tiny white tulip. But I quickly realized that this is a tough creature that must withstand a twice-daily cycle of soaking and drying, as well as a severe pounding by the surf.

Across the continent, on the remote west coast of Vancouver Island in British Columbia, I found a plant that must endure the same beating from the waves—the sea palm, a relative of kelp. These hardy plants grow only along the most exposed coasts, in the choppiest waters. Their strong holdfasts and rubbery stalklike stipes usually withstand even rough storms. On that day, however, I found dozens of the palms littering the rocks of China Beach. They had been torn loose and washed ashore during a violent storm that left a wide path of destruction.

I encountered a storm with gale-force winds along the Pacific coast of Oregon, about 250 miles south of Vancouver Island. Appropriately, I was at Cape Foulweather, and the

Cannibalistic sun star (above) attacks another starfish, clutching the prey with its rays, or arms. Rows of tube feet capped by suckers enable the 12-inch-wide star to grasp its catch. With these tubes, stars also cling to the sides of rocks and walk along the bottom. Opposite, a nudibranch perches on the upturned ray of a sea star; nearby, a hermit crab searches for food. Tiny pincers on some sea stars' backs clip off anything that tries to attach itself there, such as barnacles or other sedentary animals that need a surface to live on.

blustering winds and heavy rains there made me appreciate the implications of its name. Gray-green seas, whipped by winds into whitecaps and long plumes of spray, hurled tons of water against the craggy bluffs. Waves exploded in sudsy, billowing foam.

Watching the ocean churned into this fury, I became even more aware that the sea itself is the master craftsman of all rocky coastlines. It sculpts, cuts, and erodes the rock into fissures, caves, and arches.

This ceaseless carving creates a multitude of home-steading sites for animals suited to such harsh conditions. Most of them are found in a narrow strip called the intertidal

region, an area of rock and sand bounded by the high and low tides. Here, two diverse environments—land and sea—meet and blend. A complex variety of organisms competes for the limited space in this region. The animals tend to group into four distinct zones, spaced vertically from the high-tide mark to the low-tide mark.

Periwinkle snails and acorn barnacles live among the rocks in the splash zone, receiving occasional spray from the surf and a dousing from only the highest of tides. Just below, in the high intertidal zone, limpets, chitons, and crabs occur, and they are generally engulfed by all high tides. A variety of animals—sea stars, urchins, nudibranchs, mussels, anemones among them—prefers the middle intertidal area. This zone is usually underwater, but is exposed at low tide. In the bottom zone, the low intertidal, abalones, sea cucumbers, and octopuses flourish. They are uncovered only by the lowest of tides.

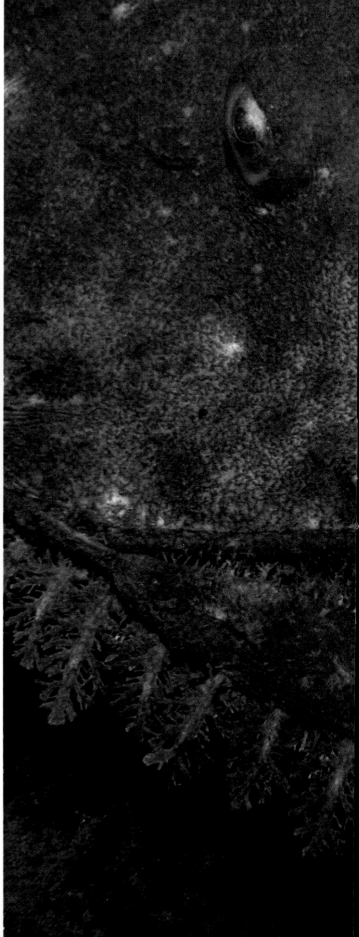

*Grotesque American
goosefish spreads the
broad, fleshy lips of its foot-
wide mouth. The fish's
mottled skin and weedlike
growths blend perfectly
with its environment—the*

*rocky ocean bottom off
Massachusetts. Delicately
branched feeding tentacles
of a sea cucumber (above)
sweep cold waters off
Maine for particles of food.
The tentacles grasp the
grains of matter and thrust
them into the large mouth
at the end of its tubular
body. By eating decaying
plants and animals, sea
cucumbers help keep rich
bottom materials recycled.*

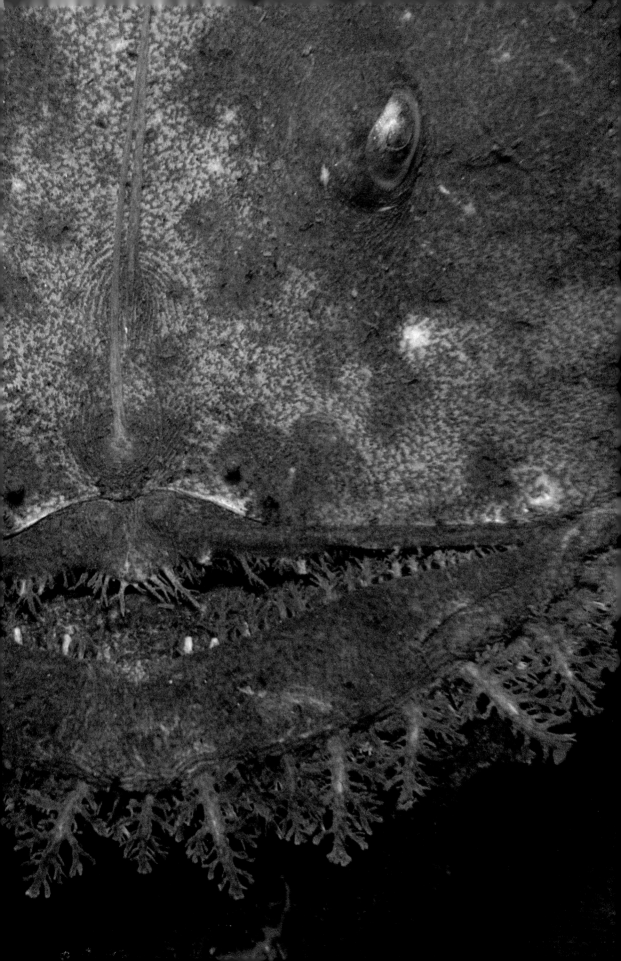

These zones form a general framework for tidal regions, and they can overlap and vary depending on conditions. Life forms can also move between two zones. Most seaweeds, for instance, grow in the two middle zones. But they provide food and shelter for animals from all four.

One moonlit night during a low tide, I investigated a tidal region along the coast of southern California that bustled with activity. Red and green rock crabs scuttled sideways and backward in every crack and crevice. Hermit crabs frantically ran to and fro on toothpick-thin legs. Anemones waved stinging tentacles that entice prey. Small fish swam from the protective coloration of the brown-red seaweeds, freezing instantly when my flashlight played on them.

In one large tidal pool, I was surprised when what I thought was a clump of seaweed slowly started moving. It passed a rock, and suddenly it looked like that rock. When it moved into open water, it took on the dark coloration around it. I finally realized that I was watching that master of camouflage, the octopus. I trained my light more directly on the elusive creature, only to have it disappear under a rock, in a crevice—I didn't know where.

Seeing, I found out, is not the only way to experience a tidal pool. I met Chris Kitting, a graduate student at Stanford University's Hopkins Marine Station in Pacific Grove, California, who is studying the foraging habits of a mollusk called the limpet.

"I follow limpets with a microphone," Chris said, "and I know what they're feeding on by the sound of the food's texture. In fact, I can even tell whether the limpets are licking or biting. One type of algae that looks like tar has a mushy sound; others snap, crackle, or pop." I was astonished when Chris played a recording of foraging limpets—it sounded like they were slowly crunching on crisp celery.

"Next time you explore at low tide take a piece of surgical tubing with you," Chris suggested. "Put one end to your ear and the other next to an animal. But don't touch it, or it might stop what it's doing."

Ignoring strange looks from other people on the beach, I knelt by the rocks with a long tube extending from my ear. At first, there was a conglomeration of unidentified sounds, but I quickly began to distinguish and separate them. I heard barnacles moving shell plates, mussels twisting on the sticky threads that attach them to rocks, crabs munching food with their strong mandibles, or jaws.

As I watched and listened to life on the rocky coasts, I found out that most of the activity there relates to finding food. Mussels and sponges strain nutrients from the water; limpets and snails scrape algae from the rocks; crabs scavenge anything, dead or alive; starfish, sea anemones, and octopuses prey on other members of the community.

To obtain food, some of these creatures are constantly on the move, some strike only when food is in sight, and some remain sedentary. But even the most sedentary

ALL BY DOUG M. WILSON

Collecting specimens for the Seattle Aquarium, biologist Kitty Nelson (above) carefully lifts a sea star from its home in Puget Sound. Other staff members (opposite) use a beach seine to gather sea life along the shores of Lopez Island. Their catch included slender, silvery sand lances—small fish that bury themselves in bottom sediment to hide.

creatures can be aggressively territorial, I learned on a crisp December afternoon during an exceptionally low tide. With Dr. Eric Hochberg, a marine biologist at the Santa Barbara Museum of Natural History, I examined sloping rocks on an isolated beach near Point Conception, California. The rocks were blanketed by hundreds of thousands of half-inch-high sea anemones jammed together in small colonies of no more than a few square feet each.

"These anemones reproduce by dividing," Eric said. "But they remain grouped together in genetically identical colonies. Look over there." He pointed to an inch-wide rift on a rock that separated two anemone colonies. "That's a

demarcation zone. Anemones of one colony respond to encroachment by members of a genetically different colony by waging territorial battles. The individuals on the outer edges of each colony are warriors, and they fight with special stinging tentacles. This aggressive behavior maintains the space between colonies." Everywhere we looked, colonies had isolated themselves by such rifts, each protecting its own territory.

As the tide began to splash higher on the sea anemones with each wave, I thought back over my explorations of the rocky coasts. I had watched a great diversity of sea creatures as they searched for food, as they played, and as they rested. Now, I had seen the results of fierce battles. My experiences with otters and lobsters, urchins and abalones, barnacles and limpets had helped me to understand the constant struggle of these creatures for survival in their harsh world.

But most important, the wonderment and joy of discovery that I had experienced as I met exotic new creatures in this rich wilderness realm would be renewed each time I poked about in a tidal pool or drifted through a kelp forest.

Bringing the ocean wilderness inside, the Seattle Aquarium provides close-range confrontations between people and marine life. Biologist Pat McMahon (above) feeds chunks of chopped squid to perch, cod, and rockfish in one section of a large community tank. From a viewing dome in the center of this tank, visitors glimpse some of the relationships of the Puget Sound ecosystem as they watch fishes, crabs, and sea urchins move around and above them. Captivated, a young boy (right) stares at an octopus clinging with five-foot-long tentacles to a wall in the tank. Bulbous head, protruding eyes, and writhing tentacles mark the octopus, one of the diverse creatures that populate the cold waters near Seattle. Children visiting the aquarium's "touch pool" handle some of the sea stars that brighten underwater landscapes of the rocky shores.

Shimmering like quicksilver, the surface of the Red Sea mirrors the jumbled face of a coral reef. Such reefs, common to shallows of tropical seas, support dazzling worlds of plant and animal life.

DAVID DOUBILET

CORAL REEFS

By Tom Melham

To dive along a coral reef is to dream—with both eyes open. You drift, soar, glide in silence through sprawling cities inhabited by millions of strange creatures. Solid rock magically billows up in fluffy thunderheads and turreted castles—or lies low in tangled, bramble-patch growths. Stair-step promontories rival the Grand Canyon's massive stone temples in color and shape.

Steep crevasses gouge the coral platform. You drop down one barely wider than yourself and, exploring its snaky contours until it grows too narrow, pass infinitely diverse coral formations. Furrowed domes of brain coral closely resemble their namesake. Wavy-edged plate corals overlap like shingles, forming pancake stacks of Paul Bunyan proportions. Staghorn corals forest the reef with stony trees. You skim their tops, watching brilliantly colored and patterned fish dart among the branches like so many tropical birds, each species extravagantly different.

All is color, form, and motion. Familiar shapes and hues align in unfamiliar ways. Tiny feather dusters and Christmas trees sprout from a rock ledge, momentarily spattering it with bright red, navy, or pink before they disappear. Violet pincushions stride slowly along the bottom. Giant bunches of broccoli glow in warm yellows and oranges.

The feather dusters and trees are really gills of burrowing worms, the pincushions are sea urchins prowling for food, and each stalk of broccoli is a colony of animals known as soft corals. Nearby, scorpion fish hide behind seaweed-like appendages, corals put forth flowery tentacles, and arrow crabs scuttle along the bottom, resembling nothing so much as church spires mounted on eight legs. Inch-long cleaner shrimp dare to enter the open jaws of coral trout 20 times their size to feed on parasites plaguing the fish. Oddities parade by endlessly; each new cranny seems to harbor an even stranger species.

The bizarre menagerie fills you with childlike fascination, perhaps evoking Saturdays once spent scrabbling through the woods in search of toadstools, stag beetles, spiderwebs. Here you feel that same sense of mystery and discovery you knew so well in youth.

To many, the word coral conjures up only images of gleaming coral jewelry—black, red, and pink. Such baubles, however, originate from marine animals that are unlike the reef builders in many ways. The red coral of the Mediterranean grows in isolated clumps, not in reefs. Ancient Greeks were among the earliest to gather it. Romans, Persians, Scythians, Indians, and Chinese also sought this rarity—for adornment, trade, or as a medicine. The Roman scholar Pliny the Elder reported that potions made of burned, powdered red coral could ease "gripings, bladder trouble and stone," and that coral amulets might protect babies from certain illnesses. He also noted—some 19 centuries ago—that continued fishing for coral had made it "very rarely to be seen in the countries where it grows."

More recent overharvesting also has depleted some beds of black coral. And in certain parts of the Pacific, excessive gathering of pink corals appears to be the cause of a gradual decline in commercial yields. All three gem corals are scarce and beautiful—but none can build reefs. The sea's vast, free-form ramparts of stone are the result of stony corals that live in shallow tropical waters in such areas as the Caribbean, the Red Sea, the tropical Indo-Pacific, and along Australia's Great Barrier Reef.

Coral reefs abound with countless surprises and apparent contradictions. They are brilliantly colored mavericks set amid the ocean's monochromes. They can survive the fury of hurricanes and hydrogen bombs (as at Bikini and Eniwetok), but will succumb to permanent temperature changes of only a few degrees. Their waters lack the huge populations of plankton that fuel most marine food webs, yet life flourishes here in greater variety than anywhere else in the sea. They grow in shallow waters accessible to man, yet they remain complex frontiers, poorly understood and continuously debated. Many experts believe reefs are currently stable worldwide—but concede that pollution and exploitation have devastated specific areas. Outwardly, the reefs seem peaceful and serene, yet they rank among the world's bloodiest battlefields, harboring sharks, barracudas, and thousands of less obvious predators.

Among the least obvious are the coral animals themselves. Many grow in delicate branching shapes, resembling trees and shrubs so closely that it's easy to see why man long considered them plants.

Greek mythology attributed corals to the seeds of seaweeds petrified by the gorgon Medusa, whose hideous face turned all who saw her to stone. Early naturalists assumed corals were some sort of marine shrub, and did little to decipher their true nature. Even the great 18th-century scientist Linnaeus seems to have believed they were plants that became animals when they flowered. Many of his contemporaries considered corals either relics of earth's primordial chaos or "zoophytes"—neither entirely animal nor entirely vegetable, but members of a separate kingdom that exhibited characteristics of both.

Only in 1726 did naturalist Jean André Peyssonnel of France show that the reef's stony forests were not plants but groups of tiny animals. The Paris Academy of Sciences found his thesis unacceptable. Peyssonnel soon left Europe for the Caribbean island of Guadeloupe, where he lived the remainder of his life as a scientist-in-exile. Even three decades later, when the Royal Society of London published his work, it suppressed his name.

Peyssonnel's critics, however, were wrong. We now know that corals—despite their sedentary nature and plant-like appearance—are animals. Although they cannot roam for food, they are voracious, agile, and efficient predators. They also manage to reproduce, to communicate, to clean

Gobies nestle among the furrows of a stony coral in the Caribbean. Almost every crevice in a coral reef provides a home or refuge for some kind of plant or animal. Billions of tiny coral polyps continuously build fortresses of limestone; these gradually form sprawling, rocky reefs that sometimes cover several miles.

*Perched on the swaying
tentacles of a sea anemone,
a cleaner shrimp waits for
passing fish. The inch-long
crustacean, when
approached, will pinch off
and eat parasites infesting
the fish. For reasons yet
undetermined, the shrimp
has an immunity to the
stinging tentacles of the
anemone. Above, feathery,
inch-high plumes of a
Christmas-tree worm rise
from a bed of coral. These
plumes trap plankton and
provide oxygen to the
animal. The worm
draws them into a
protective tube when
threatened by a predator.*

themselves, and to build reefs—all without ever moving from their rocky homes.

They begin life as free-swimming specks called planulae. Every second, billions of them course the ocean like dust motes through a shaft of sunlight. When one finds a firm foundation—a rock, a shipwreck, even a coral skeleton—it trades its wandering ways for life imprisonment, attaching permanently to the surface and becoming a mature polyp. It takes its name from the Greek word for many-footed.

Actually, it has no feet at all. Compared with animals more highly evolved, the soft-bodied polyp is not much to look at. It possesses neither legs nor fins nor face, nor even a head. It's just a fleshy sack topped by a mouth and an encircling ring of tentacles. But this simple design is a supremely successful one, having persisted some 400 million years.

One reason for this success is the polyp's remarkable ability to build its own fortress, into which it can retract. Look closely at a piece of coral rock and you'll see that it is pocked with little stars, buds, pores, or other designs. Each of these houses a single polyp. The polyp extracts calcium and carbonate ions from seawater, depositing them about itself in a close-fitting cup of solid limestone—much as an oyster manufactures mother-of-pearl. The secretions continue throughout life, providing protection and a means of growth. Limestone deposited at the base of the polyp gradually elevates the polyp itself. From this slowly rising scaffold, the ocean's tiny stonemason increases the height and thickness of its walls. Soon it splits into two polyps, then four, and so on; the individual becomes a colony.

There are three phases of coral-reef growth: polyp, colony, and reef. As colonies—each derived from a single polyp—increase in size, their stony secretions merge into many different formations—branches, plates, lobes, parapets. Eventually their polyps may number in the tens of thousands. A single reef may contain hundreds of thousands of such colonies and billions of polyps, all bound together by encrusting calcareous algae.

Colonies are primarily dead rock, veneered with only the thinnest layer of living polyps. Yet they look—and in some ways act—much like individual organisms. Often, one will crowd and eventually overtake another. "This competition for space is crucial," Dr. Yossi Loya told me in his office at Tel-Aviv University in Israel. "Corals are endlessly fighting for room; on most reefs, space, not food, is the major limiting factor of life."

When one coral overgrows another, the loser dies, and its flesh rapidly decays—but its limestone skeleton remains, appropriated by the winner as a foundation for its polyps. More aggressive corals can even extend their stomachlike mesenteries a few centimeters and digest the flesh of encroaching neighbors. Others grab for the limited space by growing faster and branching higher than their competitors. But often these large-branched

92 (Continued on page 98)

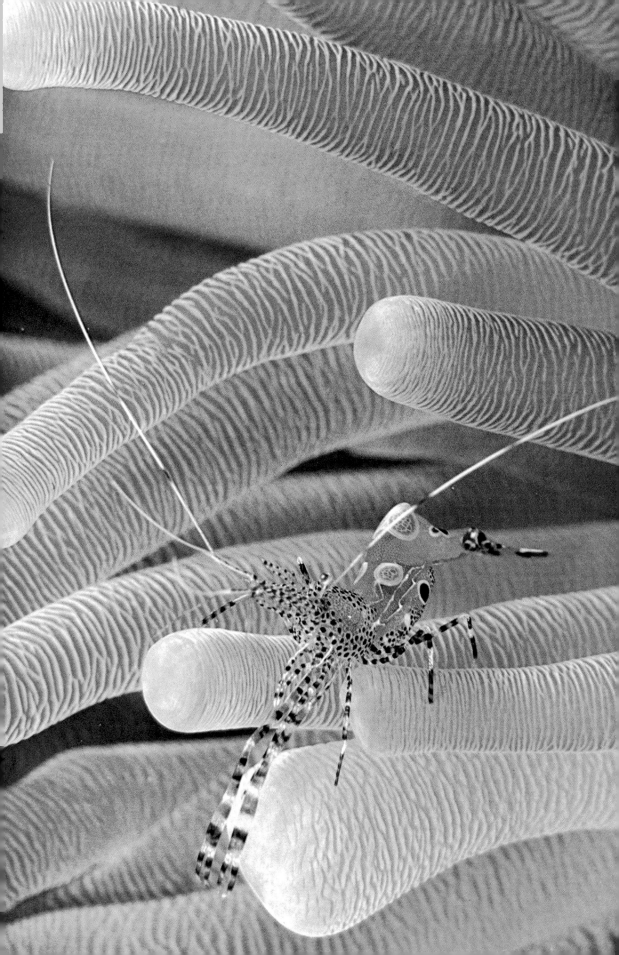

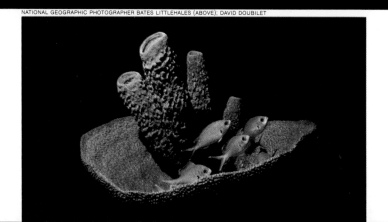

Like vases on a tray,
a cluster of tube sponges
grows from an 18-inch-
wide cup sponge in the
Caribbean. Reef-dwelling
swallowtail fish hide at
night among the sponges,
sedentary animals that
filter food from the water.

*Thirty-pound amberjacks school in the Caribbean off St.
John, one of the United States Virgin Islands. The swift
predators, each about three feet long, swim close to shore and
cruise around coral reefs to feed on smaller fishes. Like many
kinds of fishes, amberjacks do not live permanently on the
reef, but take advantage of the abundant food there. Coral
reefs in the Caribbean attract tens of thousands of divers each
year. These divers come to enjoy the wilderness beauty of the
reefs and to explore the thousands of sunken ships there.* 95

Ghostly hulk of the R.M.S. Rhone *rests 80 feet down in the Caribbean off the British Virgin Islands. In an expanse of sand, its steel hull has become an artificial reef encrusted with corals and sponges. Such creatures attach themselves to anything clean and solid—a rock, another coral, or a shipwreck. The* Rhone, *a British mail packet, foundered during a hurricane in 1867; it sank with thousands of dollars' worth of gold bullion and specie—and a loss of 123 lives. Like a sunburst, a school of grunts (above) swims past a hole in the hull of the sunken ship. At top, sea fans, a type of flexible coral, gently wave in the current.*

varieties become top-heavy; like giant oaks, they may topple in storms. Their broken portions may then support new coral planulae and limestone-secreting algae, and the cycle continues. Growth, decay, and regrowth repeat endlessly as the reef buttresses itself with its own detritus.

The overwhelming bulk of this lively submarine metropolis is, like its component colonies, lifeless rock. It represents the combined debris of untold billions of corals, algae, shellfish, and other organisms, all cemented together and steadily compacted into a mass that can be several miles long and thousands of feet thick. But only its surface lives.

Without that surface, reefs would lack color as well as life, since their bare limestone skeletons are almost always white—unlike the pigmented remains of gem corals. It is the polyps' tissue that colors stony corals with every hue in the spectrum. Most are pastel, but some glow fiery red or dusky purple. Even so, daytime visitors to the reef's flowery gardens usually see only pale imitations of their true colors—because most coral polyps are nocturnal, withdrawing deep within their skeletal residences by day. To see the polyps bloom, you must dive the reef after dark.

Plunge into the liquid blackness and, as the bubbles noisily clear, drift without lights. You're in a void, insulated from the rest of the world. Your senses strain for signals. You stare but see only black in all directions. You feel nothing, taste or smell nothing, and hear nothing except your own breathing. You flow with the current, unable to tell in which direction you are moving or what lies ahead—and you wonder how fish can navigate at night.

Perhaps some are following you right now. Reef sharks might be on the prowl—they roam at night—or even giant groupers. They can weigh more than 600 pounds and have mouths like caverns. You recall the day on Australia's Great Barrier Reef when a fellow diver speared a large coral trout—and then saw a huge grouper loom up out of the darkness below. Thinking to appease the beast, the diver let go his catch—but the grouper ignored it and kept coming. The diver was in full retreat when his terrifying pursuer caught up and took a gulp that sucked both swim fins right off his feet! In only a few milliseconds, the diver broke the surface and jumped into his boat.

A fish like that might be homing in on *you* right now. It's getting closer. Closer still.

Time to switch on the waterproof lamp.

Its yellowish tunnel of light plays across the reef hurriedly, and you see—with great relief—no monster fish. But look at the colors! Before you stretches a world transformed—random splashes of pigment everywhere. You feel a surge of discovery, much like the one experienced by archeologist Howard Carter when his flickering candle first probed the dark recesses of King Tut's tomb:

"At first I could see nothing, . . . but presently, as my

With sinuous coils, a branch of whip coral 14 feet long extends from a reef 80 feet down in the Red Sea. Craftsmen in the Pacific use such black coral to make bracelets.

eyes grew accustomed to the light, details . . . emerged slowly from the mist, strange animals. . . . I was struck dumb with amazement, and when Lord Carnarvon, unable to stand the suspense any longer, inquired anxiously, 'Can you see anything?' it was all I could do to get out the words, 'Yes, wonderful things.' "

At a distance the corals seem smudged and fuzzy; closer in, that fuzziness resolves into a shimmering fringe of polyps, extended and swaying like flowers in a breeze. Their delicate petals are the tentacles, outrageously colored in various shades of mauve, yellow, olive, red, pale blue. Brilliant red-orange ones blaze atop a colony like miniature flames.

But the longer you watch, the more this flower garden reveals itself as a deadly network of grasping, many-fingered hands. Each polyp, coated with glue-like mucus, opens and closes ceaselessly, trapping plankton that well up from the seafloor with nightly temperature changes. Groups of stinging cells, far too small to penetrate your skin or even to be seen without a microscope, assist the polyp's sticky fingers by stunning prey. The tentacles then pass their catch from one to another in bucket-brigade fashion, toward the animal's centrally located mouth. Some large coral polyps are so powerful and adept that, like the closely related but much larger sea anemones, they even snare small fish.

Touch a coral polyp and it retracts into its stone cup. Tap it harder and its neighbors also go into hiding. Harder still and the entire colony may withdraw. Through a network of nerves, each polyp, although independent and locked in stone, communicates with other colony members. Polyps also cleanse themselves of ocean-borne sand and other debris. Tiny, hairlike cilia covering their bodies waft in concert like miniature tentacles, moving sediment toward the edges of the colony. Unusually thick accumulations of silt stimulate corals to secrete an insulating layer of mucus, which traps the dirt. It is later sloughed off the reef in translucent sheets.

This purging tactic not only prevents corals from being buried but also provides other reef residents with an additional food source—the protein-rich mucus.

Some large solitary corals living on sandy seafloors possess a talent even more phenomenal for a sedentary creature, marine biologist Lev Fishelson told me. "If one of these polyps is hurled upside down onto the sandy bottom, it can right itself," he said. "Tentacles along one side of the polyp excavate the sand below until the coral's position becomes so undermined that it begins to tilt. Continued selective digging by the tentacles eventually turns the entire polyp right side up. How the polyp knows which side should dig and which should not remains a mystery, but it's an incredible example of coral survival."

Corals, however, are but one wonder of the night reef. Droves of conchs and sea urchins (Continued on page 106)

Scattering hunks of coral debris to form a shallow depression, an 18-inch-long triggerfish prepares a nest on a reef in the Red Sea. A female will soon deposit her eggs there, and the male will guard them until they hatch. Coral reefs attract hundreds of species of animals to feed, breed, and sleep. They populate entire reefs—the flat crowns as well as the walls that slope down to the depths. Some creatures— sponges, mollusks, and marine worms—even burrow into the solid limestone of the reefs.

Contorted fingers of a red sponge and the intricate lace of a black coral jut from the wall of a reef in the Red Sea. Both animals grow out from the dark rock toward the sunlight. The Red Sea, abounding with coral reefs, fills a rift zone separating Africa and Asia. In some places the narrow body of water drops abruptly to depths of 6,000 feet or more. Stony corals grow only along the topmost fringes of the walls. Above, a squirrelfish spends the day concealed in a rock crevice, emerging at night to hunt. A hawkfish (below) hovers among coral fronds, its mouth open to capture tiny animals that drift with the currents. The regular pattern of this three-inch-long fish matches that of the coral. A grouper, one of the most predominant reef predators, lurks behind a red sponge. Overleaf: A lionfish spreads featherlike fins. Sharp dorsal spines charged with poison protect the foot-long fish.

101

Slender barracudas band together 120 feet down in the Red Sea. Like silvery darts, the three-foot-long predators strike prey with lightning-fast bursts of speed. A conspicuously striped clownfish (below) nestles safely among the stinging tentacles of a cluster of sea anemones. Marine biologists believe that these small fish gradually gain protection from the anemones' poison by rubbing increasingly larger areas of their bodies against the writhing tentacles. Proximity to the deadly anemones offers the clownfish protection from predators. In turn, the fish may bring crustaceans and other bits of food to the anemones. At bottom, showy butterfly fish with pointed snouts poke into a creviced reef wall, searching for food.

desert their daytime hiding spots to march boldly across the reef. Lacking limbs, urchins walk on the tips of their spines, which also serve for defense and as levers to right them when they're overturned. If disturbed, an urchin waves its spines, giving the appearance of a blind man armed with a thousand canes, tap-tapping in all directions to determine his whereabouts. Indeed, these creatures have no eyes.

Night also brings out sun-shy lobsters, moray eels, and many-armed brittle stars. Sleeping fishes hang motionless under coral ledges or just off the bottom, comatose in spite of their open, lidless eyes. Some hide in packets of their own mucus that may prevent their scent from alerting predators. Many others wear nighttime colors and patterns dramatically altered from those of day.

Your lamp loses brilliance and seems to falter. The problem, fortunately, is biological and not mechanical. Thousands of half-inch-long fry swarm around the lens like insects charging a camp lantern. They're startlingly fast and densely packed. Move as you will, they cling to the beam.

A similar persistence pervades all levels of reef life. The combination of limited space and huge numbers of creatures often makes for intense competition, both among individuals and among species. Even the simplest events may have far-reaching consequences, because the actions of one organism touch the lives of so many others. Consider the rainbow-hued parrotfish grazing on a stretch of coral reef with comical, bucktoothed jaws. You're witnessing much more than the obvious life-and-death drama of one animal feeding at another's expense.

Its teeth scrape the reef surface for food, gouging the underlying rock. Limestone is broken up and passed out as sand—the same white sand that accumulates in beaches ringing so many tropical islands. Parrotfish produce countless tons of it each year. It's an important commodity to reef dwellers. This sand, combined with the remains of calcareous algae, collects on the bottom. Sea cucumbers and other scavengers sift it for organic nutrients; stingrays forage in it for shrimp and crabs; fishes burrow into it at night to escape nocturnal predators; storms and ocean currents rework it into sandbars, shoals, and even islands. Most coral cays are simply sand that has been piled up, fertilized by the droppings of ocean birds, and colonized by waterborne seeds.

Usually, the damage that the parrotfish causes to a colony of coral is negligible. Polyps overgrow small bare spots quickly. Yet if the wound is extensive, or the coral is a slow-growing variety, that scar may become a doorway for multitudes of tiny organisms. Burrowing sponges, marine worms, and mollusks enter the rock, now unprotected by its veneer of polyps. Like termites in a fallen tree, they lace it with endless mazes. Eventually, the weakened colony collapses, even though living polyps still cover most of it. If the fallen pieces lodge in some crevice, calcareous algae may

Cloaked with spots, a sweetlips opens its mouth so a striped cleaner wrasse can eat parasites and dead or diseased tissue. Many wrasses wear bright colors and distinctive markings for quick recognition by fish that need their cleaning services.

alight, secrete limestone over them, and reincorporate them into the reef. But if the coral fragments fall on sand, ocean currents probably will roll them about, killing the polyps. The rock speedily decays, releasing calcium and carbonate ions back to the seawater in a dust-to-dust cycle that ensures an unfailing supply for future generations.

But even here the parrotfish story does not end. The collapse of one part of a reef exposes the rest of it to more borers and parasites. Holes form; the once-solid platform may slowly become a giant sponge cake. Gaps and tunnels provide innumerable hiding places for all sizes of fishes and other creatures, enabling the same volume of rock to sup-

port more individuals. The openings also encourage a greater variety of species, for they represent new environmental niches. Shadowy holes shunned by the upper reef's light-loving organisms become catch basins for reef detritus and protective crevices for lobsters and other bottom life.

In nature each species thrives within a particular range of environments. Many tolerate less-than-perfect conditions, so long as they don't have to compete with better-adapted creatures. But the reef's staggering competition for food and space has filled it with highly specialized organisms. Each is well suited to the narrow limits of its particular mini-environment, so well suited, in fact, that it often cannot survive even slight differences in conditions.

Tiny changes in food supply, available light, or other environmental factors can give one creature the edge it needs to proliferate—and doom another. A coral colony that gradually grows into the stream of a small ocean current will divert that flow of water—and slightly alter that section of reef. As the colony snatches plankton from the current in ever-increasing amounts, nearby corals—now denied their usual food supply—wither like crops during a drought.

Camouflaged shrimp (above, left) hides among the arms of a feather star on a crowded coral reef off Australia. The feather star uses small claws to attach itself to the limestone. Another shrimp hangs among the polyps of a soft coral. Both species of shrimp find safety in their ability to mimic their surroundings.

Different species, better attuned to the new environmental conditions, will then take over.

Despite the reef's raging competition, however, many of its creatures find mutual advantage in each other. Needle-nosed trumpetfish often hide behind bulkier fish and dart from behind them to strike their bottom-dwelling prey. Even coral polyps rely on other life forms for their growth and survival, harboring within their very tissue unicellular algae that are as essential to the reef as is the coral itself.

Dr. Dennis Taylor, an algal physiologist studying symbiotic associations at the University of Miami, told me about these tiny algae, known as zooxanthellae. "In a way still not completely understood, they help the polyps secrete their limestone skeletons. By converting sunlight, carbon dioxide, and water into food, zooxanthellae provide the coral with oxygen, organic nutrients, and the necessary additional energy required to build their rock walls.

"As in any symbiotic association, the algae get something in return. They receive important nutrients from the coral as well as the carbon dioxide that is needed in photosynthesis. They also live within the protection of the coral's limestone walls." Obviously, the coral-zooxanthellae association is a cozy one, and countless others, similarly complex, make the reef a tightly knit tapestry of life.

Although most colonies of coral continue to grow as long as they live, their range is extremely limited. They cannot tolerate dirty or deep waters that would bar sunlight from reaching the zooxanthellae; their calcification process requires water temperatures above 68° F. Thus the reef-building corals are restricted almost exclusively to clear, shallow tropical seas. Striking similarities in reef life and formation exist around the world, although the reefs in the Caribbean Sea and the western Atlantic are generally smaller in extent and have fewer species of coral than the reefs in the Pacific and Indian oceans.

The proximity of the Caribbean reefs to the United States makes them a favorite of American divers, who each year flock to tropical islands there in the tens of thousands. Dozens of dive spots in the Caribbean bear labels that read like the names of ski slopes: Valley of the Dolls, Little Drop-off, Pipeline, Cinderella Castle, Three Sisters, Big Tunnel, The Wall. An accompanying spate of dive shops reflects the growing popularity of sport diving in a place known not only for its beautiful coral formations but also for its many sunken ships.

Hurricanes and coral reefs have made the Caribbean one of the world's major nautical graveyards. Spanish treasure fleets foundered there with the spoils of conquered empires. Frigates and merchant vessels, steamers and square-riggers also went down. In the five centuries since Columbus first visited them, these reefs have claimed thousands of ships. Although many have rotted into nonexistence, others retain something of their original shape—and consistently lure divers, just as the Acropolis draws yearly crowds to Athens.

A special favorite over the years is R.M.S. *Rhone*, a steel-hulled, 19th-century British mail packet that ran aground off the Virgin Islands in a storm on October 29, 1867. Even today, divers sometimes find bottles and china plates bearing the ship's monogram. Hollywood film crews thought enough of *Rhone*'s ghostly profile to cast her as *Goliath*, a fictional wreck that provided the stage for undersea battles in the 1977 thriller, "The Deep."

As you slowly descend 30 feet below the surface, a massive stern propeller materializes out of the greenish haze.

You pass great hatchways and steel eyes a foot in diameter—and recognize the twisted form ahead as a section of hull, heeled sharply to starboard on its sea of sand. Bright corals, sponges, algae, and other colorful growths encrust the wreck with a mini-reef. Fishes drift around and through it in diffuse schools that coalesce and disperse like dreams. Ironically, the *Rhone*'s carcass supports an oasis of life that otherwise would not exist; the sand alone here is too unstable for corals and other organisms to colonize. This thick blanket of overgrowth gives *Rhone* a wild appearance. At first glance it seems to be a virgin wreck, undisturbed during its more than a century of submergence. The urge to explore tugs you closer.

You enter the bow section and look up to see inch-long flashes of color—tropical fishes, skimming over the growths that mask *Rhone*'s steel. They never roam far from the reef surface. Where it follows the upward bend of the hull, they swim vertically. Overhead, they hang upside down.

The fish-dappled ceiling also gleams with what appear to be gravity-defying puddles   *(Continued on page 116)*

Sand-fringed speck of land in a realm of coral, One Tree Island reaches above a wave-lashed section of Australia's Great Barrier Reef. Largest complex of reefs in the world, the Great Barrier extends more than 1,250 miles along the east coast of Australia. Some 350 species of coral helped build this largely unexplored group of reefs, coral cays, and islands.

Embraced by a tube coral polyp along the Great Barrier Reef, a young silverside fish struggles to free itself. The fish eventually succumbed to the paralyzing effect of poison-tipped cells studding the tentacles of the half-inch-wide polyp. Nocturnal feeders, these corals subsist on a diet of plankton—and an occasional small fish or worm. Most corals remain within their limestone fortresses during the day; but even there, they fall prey to some creatures. Below, a crown-of-thorns starfish feeds on coral polyps by engulfing them with its stomach. The spiny-armed starfish leaves behind only empty coral skeletons. An infestation of crown-of-thorns starfish beginning in the 1960's ravaged portions of the Great Barrier and other reefs in the Pacific. A few scientists feared that the starfish would destroy some of the reefs. But the booming population of crown-of-thorns returned to a more normal level, and the reefs have regenerated. Fossil evidence indicates that such explosions in the numbers of crown-of-thorns starfish occur in natural cycles.

CARL ROESSLER (ABOVE); AL GIDDINGS, SEA FILMS, INC. (BELOW); BEN CROPP

Fearsome great white shark slowly cruises
Pacific waters off southern Australia,
hunting for food. With jagged two-inch
teeth, the 15-foot-long predator can tear
huge chunks of flesh from its prey. Like a
giant butterfly, a manta ray with a
wingspread of 12 feet (below) glides
gracefully along the Great Barrier Reef in
search of plankton. A remora, a fish that
eats the same food as the ray and also gains
protection from it, clings by means of a
large sucker to the underside of the
thousand-pound beast. Below, left, a diver
in the Coral Sea off Australia reaches for
a sea snake swiftly propelling itself with
a paddlelike tail. Among the world's
most deadly animals, sea snakes kill
with poison injected from sharp fangs.

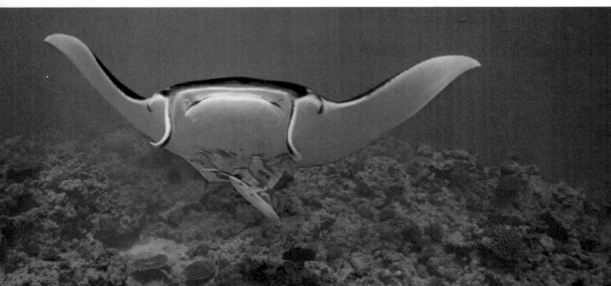

Its home a spotted castle, a tiger cowrie (right) scours a reef in the Philippines, scooping up algae and minute crustaceans. The mollusk's knobby, translucent mantle extends like a frilly petticoat. The mantle, a specialized organ, secretes a limy substance that creates and constantly strengthens the cowrie's five-inch-long shell. Below, a cowrie senses its way with pointed tentacles; tiny eyes peer from under the stalks. Reclusive animals, cowries hide in coral rubble during the day and feed at night.

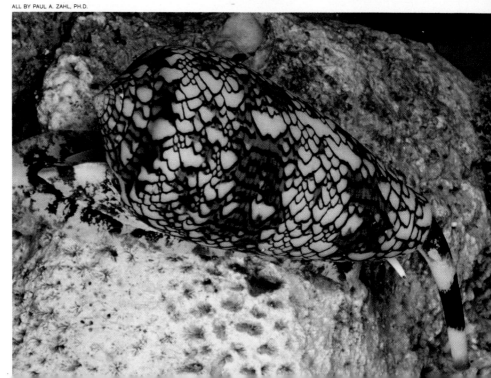

Intricately patterned textile cone (far left) probes a coral reef in the Philippines with its ringed siphon. The organ, which retracts into the shell (left), serves as a sensor. It also draws in water from which the cone obtains oxygen. Poisonous, textile cones kill other mollusks for food, using barbed, needle-sharp teeth that inject a paralyzing venom. The four-inch-long cones usually live in sandy patches on coral reefs, where they bury themselves during the day, emerging only at night to stalk prey.

of mercury. You poke one with a finger, but it lacks substance. Each puddle is merely a silvery air bubble trapped by the overhanging ledge and flattened by water pressure.

Their presence is proof that you are not the first visitor here. Thousands of preceding divers have left their quicksilver exhalations within *Rhone*. Still, there's something magnetic about a wreck, even an oft-visited one. And *Rhone* has an extra attraction—she was carrying a fortune in gold bullion and specie on her ill-fated voyage. Salvors in the 1870's removed thousands of dollars' worth, but who knows? They may have missed a few loose bars. Recently, one diver found a gold coin lying on the seafloor. It had been uncovered by the currents that constantly sweep the sand. You may have similar luck.

You scan the bottom for odd shapes that might betray bits of the *Rhone*'s hoard. Ten minutes of scrounging reveals a treasure of sorts—a tiny medicine jar and splinters of china that originally outfitted the vessel. But there are also less ancient souvenirs: twist-cap bottles, flash bulbs, corroded batteries, and two algae-encrusted snorkels. No matter; if it's gold you're after, there are many more wrecks to search and rumors to follow up. After all, this is the history-heavy Caribbean, haunt of buccaneers and nemesis of treasure-laden Spanish galleons.

Not far from *Rhone* rises the tiny uninhabited island of Dead Chest—sometimes called Dead Man's Chest—which may have inspired the famous pirate ditty:

Fifteen men on The Dead Man's Chest—
Yo-ho-ho, and a bottle of rum!

Chanted by retired pirate Billy Bones in Robert Louis Stevenson's classic, *Treasure Island*, the song purportedly refers to the time the villainous Edward Teach—Blackbeard—decided to discipline 15 members of his crew. He marooned them on Dead Chest with nothing but a cutlass and a bottle of rum. True or not, this romantic tale persists, as do other stories of pirate plunder and sunken treasure.

Anegada, the easternmost of the British Virgin Islands, borders deadly Horse Shoe Reef, tomb for about 200 vessels, one dating to the 16th century. Many a wreck was scavenged by the islanders as soon as the ship ran aground. Others escaped that fate only to be buried by the shifting sands. Dozens of hulks have never been found—and could be uncovered by just the right storm.

Today, most residents of this coral cay, which stands only 25 feet above sea level at its highest point, regularly fish its coral barriers; a few dive there. But Horse Shoe curves away from Anegada for some ten miles, creating an immense search area for salvors. Even so, you can't help feeling your own temperature rise one stickily warm evening on Anegada as you realize the local fishermen at the next table *aren't* talking about fish. Their singsong, West Indian lilt colors the conversation:

DOUGLAS FAULKNER

Lacy fan of a coral captures drifting food off the Palau Islands in the western Pacific. Polyps line the branches of this delicate colony of animals. Coralline algae (opposite, upper) splotch a reef near Palau with pinks and greens. Halimeda (opposite, lower) spreads segmented fronds at the bottom of Truk Lagoon in the Pacific. Such calcareous algae decay into a thick carpet on the bottom, providing shelter for many reef creatures.

Lowell: Da big one, mon, you know he *always* gets away.

Clinton: Ya mon, I uz out on no'th side, divin' fo' lobsters. Saw dis wreck wid a big metal chest, big as a fridge. Thought, next time out here, mon, gonna take a look at dat chest.

Lowell: Ya?

Clinton: Dat uz four, five year ago. Nevah been able to find it since.

Silence and faraway looks follow, but only momentarily. Soon the friendly banter again picks up, punctuated by table-thumping laughter and exciting talk of past "finds" on the reef. As with all good tales, you're never sure whether they're true.

But they're certainly tempting. Before you decide to seek out Clinton's fridge-size chest, however, remember that few treasure hunters have made it pay. The vast majority find only failure. On the reef, nature's treasures are infinitely more plentiful and accessible than man's.

This is especially true of the world's most famous coral complex: Australia's Great Barrier Reef. Not a continuous single reef but a myriad collection of barrier reefs, coral cays, and rock islands all interlaced with lagoons and fringing reefs, the Great Barrier stretches some 1,250 miles off the coast of Queensland. For all its fame, however, it remains remarkably unspoiled and undeveloped. Not one dive shop is located on its spectacular outer barrier. None of the world's reefs is wilder or more mysterious.

Although man has known about the Great Barrier for more than 200 years, he still understands little of its workings. Scientists aren't even sure exactly which corals grow there, not to mention other life forms and how they interact.

"Incredibly little research has been done," Dr. J. E. Veron told me in his office at the Australian Institute of Marine Science near Townsville. Veron and his colleague Dr. Michel Pichon, however, have embarked on a first step—cataloging the reef's resident corals.

"It's extraordinary it hasn't been done before," Veron added. "Of course, the job's enormous. Looking back, I don't think I would have started, knowing what I do now. But it has to be done."

He picked up two of his 12,000 coral specimens—one a ripply plate, the other treelike.

"These are both the same species. Corals are not like birds or other animals—you can't always tell them by their shape. Early naturalists didn't realize this and simply gave a new name to every coral that looked different from others; that's why coral taxonomy has been such a mess."

A card file in Veron's office contains all scientific names ever given to Australian corals—about 4,000. In reality, probably only 350 distinct coral species live here. But even so, that's several times the number known in the Caribbean. The Great Barrier Reef's other creatures are equally diverse—all of which makes for a puzzling and terribly complex realm.

117

Recent confusion over *Acanthaster planci*—the notorious crown-of-thorns starfish—is a case in point. Crown-of-thorns eat coral polyps. Usually their populations are so widely scattered that the corals' normal growth and regeneration more than offset any damage done. But in the 1960's dense aggregations of *Acanthaster* suddenly began to infest many coral reefs, stripping them in places of polyps. The ravaged coral skeletons soon decayed or became overgrown with algae.

Panic set in on shore, as some people warned of catastrophic erosion and other environmental disasters that would plague an Australia deprived of its vast coral rampart. Some biologists blamed man for the apparent calamity. The crown-of-thorns' main natural enemy, a whelk named triton, long had been overharvested for its pretty trumpet-shaped shell. Hurriedly, programs to control *Acanthaster* took shape. Volunteers went about the reefs, removing and killing starfish or injecting them with doses of formalin, a deadly poison.

Today, the crown-of-thorns have returned to more normal concentrations, and the reefs again seem secure—but probably not because of man's efforts. Geologist Edgar Frankel of the University of Sydney recently discovered evidence of past *Acanthaster* population explosions in the reef's fossil record—indicating that such blooms and retrenchments are part of some natural cycle.

Much of Australia's intriguing reef life also flourishes in other tropical reaches of the Indo-Pacific region, luring scientists as well as sport divers. Some areas, such as the Red Sea's Gulf of Aqaba, offer not only the Great Barrier Reef's beauty but also the Caribbean's accessibility. Because Aqaba occupies a steep rift valley, its reefs often drop straight down for thousands of feet—only a few dozen yards from shore. Such walls represent the ragged boundary of the reef, where the sea's destructive forces balance coral growth. Here, corals take on their most spectacular shapes and do their most prolific blossoming.

Along one such seaward edge you peer down stone walls that plummet vertically much farther than you can see. The water before you gleams with a surreal cobalt color, signaling its abyssal depth.

A self-protective desire to return to the shallows struggles briefly with the irresistible urge to explore. Rationality loses; you drift out beyond the cliff top and, with an eagle's freedom, take the plunge.

Dropping like a rock or cruising in slow spirals, you head down past lofty stone battlements dramatically cut and sculpted. Silvery fishes hang in vertical schools, veiling the crags with living curtains that waft gently in the invisible surge. The fact that water absorbs sunlight causes yet another surprise: Colors disappear one by one as increasing depth steals light of varying wavelengths. Red is the first to go—nick a finger below 30 feet and it oozes green blood. You

Industrious polyps build coral gardens in an astonishing spectrum of shapes and sizes. Branches of staghorn coral (upper) sprout in a clump nearly two feet wide. Dimpled columns of another stony coral (lower) resemble stubby fingers.

begin to wonder just what colors the creatures before you *really* are.

No matter how deep you venture, the water's bottomless blue persists, luring you ever downward with foglike mystery. Above stretches the ocean's rumpled surface, silhouetting the coral towers with great golden shafts of light. You have entered one of nature's cathedrals. Like its Gothic counterparts, it is tall, dark, awesome; you feel dwarfed by its size and uplifted by the cascades of light.

Suddenly you sense, rather than see, a shadow pass overhead. You look up—and see the blood-freezing profile of a hammerhead shark, perhaps 12 feet long. Tingles of fear race through your body as you realize, vividly, how clumsy and helpless man truly is in water. Fortunately, the shark is distant—and disinterested. Fear quickly fades to awe as this creature with the ugly head performs a most beautiful ballet. Its fluid motions possess the grace and raw power of a soaring condor or a cheetah on the run. Killer, you say? To be sure—but like barracudas and morays, sharks are much maligned. They rarely molest humans without provocation.

The hammerhead deftly cruises around a coral parapet and is gone. Strangely, you feel disappointment, not relief. Like all good performers, it has made its exit a touch too soon, leaving the audience wishing for an encore.

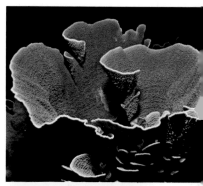

Encores abound throughout the reef, for this is a realm of many show-offs. Two spotted eagle rays wing past majestically, like swans in flight. A sea turtle clings to a nearby promontory, then darts off into the dimness. Dolphins cavort offshore. Somewhere on the reef flat above, parrotfish munch coral rock, and barracudas munch parrotfish.

Just below the water's surface, too far away for you to see, armadas of translucent jellyfish converge near the reef edge. You ascend unknowingly into their midst. Suddenly you see them, thousands of them, all heading straight at you, streaming over, under, and around—like flying saucers in a science-fiction movie. They're automatons, each pulsing rhythmically, silently. One accidentally impales itself on a sea urchin's spines but stubbornly keeps pulsing, showing a determination symbolic of the reef and of life itself. Eventually it rolls off the spines and continues its journey. You dodge its nebulous companions as you surface, successfully avoiding the stings but falling prey to a much more prevalent hazard of reefs—the tendency to blabber about what you've just seen.

Toweling off with other divers, you find it hard not to compare observations and even harder to understand how anyone could choose to go through life without experiencing the reef's magic. Its spell is every bit as potent as that cast by the shadows in a redwood forest, by sunrise gilding a snowcapped mountain, by a glacier's barren expanse, or by the fiery colors of a New England autumn. Quite simply, the living reef is one of nature's great wildernesses—and a source of enduring satisfaction to man's soul.

In tranquil Pacific waters near Palau, fragile plate coral (upper) grows in a flowing three-foot-wide spiral. Swirling ridges mark the separate rows of living polyps in a three-foot-high formation of Pachyseris *coral (lower).*

119

Giant clam, nestled among corals on a reef in the
Palau Islands, gently spreads its fringed shells.
The ten-inch-long clam siphons water into its
body, then filters food from it. Almost invisible,
a scorpion fish (below) waits for prey. Poisonous
dorsal spines—used for protection—make this
one of the Pacific's most feared species. At
bottom, a parrotfish sleeps in a cocoon of mucus.
Some marine biologists believe that the covering
protects the fish from predators as it sleeps. With
beaklike teeth, parrotfish scrape the surface of the
reef for algae; some species also eat coral polyps.

THE

Filigree of sargassum weed filters bright sunlight in the Atlantic Ocean. Such vegetation, rare in the immensity of the open sea, provides food and shelter for a school of young jacks.

DAVID DOUBILET

OPEN OCEAN

By Tee Loftin

"Exploring the open ocean is like hiking through a desert wilderness instead of walking down a crowded city street," said marine biologist Alice Alldredge. "Compared with the teeming life of a coral reef, the open sea seems vacant. Large creatures such as sharks, whales, tuna, and squids swim by only occasionally, and even the tiny bits of life are scattered. Plankton, the small drifting plants and animals that are abundant in all waters, appear in concentrations averaging about one-tenth those of other areas."

I talked with Dr. Alldredge, a dark-haired young woman, in her office at the University of California, Santa Barbara. Her specialty is zooplankton, the animal drifters. She has pursued these small creatures, studying, counting, and bottling them during more than 500 dives in the open ocean—that great sprawl of water that lies far beyond the sight of land and far above the ocean floor. Such empty expanses are marked by a lack of interaction between shore and water, surface and bottom.

"When I'm out in the middle of the Pacific Ocean on a dive to observe zooplankton, I like to imagine I'm one of them, just hanging weightless in the open sea," Alice continued. "I drift with the creatures some 30 to 60 feet below the surface. In this quiet layer we're out of the rough motion of surface water, but we still benefit from the light of the sun. It's a silent realm with no horizons, no boundaries. My body shifts with the currents. I'm suspended in clear blue water, far above the cold, black abyss.

"I simply wait for zooplankton to pass by. Perhaps I'll spot a giant jellyfish with long tentacles dangling behind it, or a half-inch-long lobster larva, or a snail with wings made of transparent tissue. All these creatures hunt and eat each other or search for phytoplankton—small drifting plants—in the water."

In the open sea many of the zooplankton are gelatinous, draped with intricate webs of jellylike mucus that break apart in rougher waters near shore. These webs, which can be whimsically beautiful, serve as buoyant balloons, floating houses, netlike cones—all rafts that keep the creatures from sinking into the deep. They also double as gatherers of food; some trap, some strain, some enfold.

"Although these mucus webs might be several feet in extent, they're transparent and therefore hard to see," Alice continued. "Once you've spotted one of these creatures, you can't afford to take your eyes off it—or even blink—or you might lose it.

"When I've found an animal, I'll follow it around for as long as I can. Since I can't take notes, I carry a tape recorder with a microphone attached to my throat against my vocal cords. Generally my observations are on what's happening to the creature: 'It's traveled two feet in 30 seconds' or 'It's moving a gelatinous wing to draw in phytoplankton.' A major part of my studies concerns who is eating whom, which is much of what life in the sea is all about."

Alice is one of the pioneers in observing open-sea plankton in their own world. She worked with Dr. William Hamner, then of the University of California, Davis, who developed the technique in the early 1970's. Before then researchers studied life that was caught in nets, and the gelatinous zooplankton would break apart into tiny blobs or be badly damaged when they were caught. Only in the last few years have scientists begun to uncover the mysteries of these open-sea plankton.

"The waters of the open sea are almost always clear, reflecting blue, the color they least readily absorb," Alice told me in her office overlooking a seaweed-strewn beach. "But clear water is often empty water. No bottom sediment or nutrient-rich mud from rivers. No green-yellow clouds of algae or flowerlike diatoms. No crowds of zooplankton. When I move out with the open-sea drifters, I see individuals just every so often.

"One of my favorites is the foot-long Venus's girdle, which glides through the water with ribbonlike wings. Other favorites are the salps, barrel-shaped transparent creatures that are joined together with others of their kind to form long chains. I saw one salp chain that would spiral around this office several times.

"One of the most striking creatures I've come across was a siphonophore, a bizarre animal with a gas-filled bag. It was at least 80 feet in length, and dangled long stinging tentacles. I've had a lot of experiences in the open ocean, but one thing I would love to see is a cloud of these siphonophores rising past me from the depths. They come to the surface at night to feed on tiny animals, and then, before dawn, they empty their gas bags and sink back down."

Sinking is the ultimate fate of everything in the open sea. Plants, animals, nutrients, waste matter all eventually fall to the bottom. But that bottom is so far down that it may take weeks, or even months, to reach. And often storms or upwelling currents sweep the material back toward the warm surface where it decomposes more quickly and provides more nutrients.

"Storms keep the web of life vibrant in the open sea," Alice said. "Hurricanes can stir water and the life forms in it to depths of 200 feet. Even a steady wind can push aside surface water, allowing a tongue of deeper, colder water to sweep up and take its place. During one of my dives, a cone of cold water suddenly came from below and engulfed me. It carried marine snow—bits of matter that are in the process of decomposing."

In the spring steady winds that stir nutrients combine with the longer periods of sunshine to cause the sea to bloom. All life forms reproduce suddenly and at a fantastic rate. Every day for about two months, each tiny plant divides, creating vast new populations. Because of the newly available food, the zooplankton begin to feast, and then they start multiplying, too. Small fish (Continued on page 130)

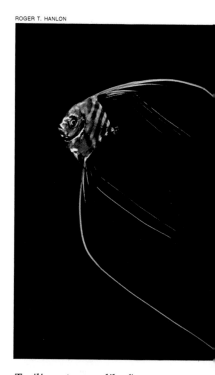

ROGER T. HANLON

Trailing streamerlike fins, an African pompano glides through Caribbean waters. The five-inch-long fish uses the graceful appendages as stabilizers. This pompano, like all creatures of the open ocean, must constantly hunt food. Lacking abundant nutrients, the empty expanses support one-tenth the life found elsewhere.

Masters of camouflage, creatures of the Sargasso Sea—a sprawling region of doldrums in the Atlantic—have adopted the shape and coloration of the predominant sargassum weed there. The olive and gold tendrils of the seaweed, buoyed by pea-size bladders, nurture dozens of marine species. A six-inch-long pipefish (right) hangs motionless among the sargassum fronds. At top, left, a sargassum fish swallows a filefish, visible through the translucent lower jaw. The three-inch-long sargassum fish has leafy appendages that resemble the blades of the weed. An inch-long crab (top, right) waits for prey. The Sargasso Sea makes a perfect refuge for such creatures. Circulating currents of wind and water have isolated a 50,000-square-mile zone of quiet that resembles the hole of a giant doughnut. Because of the lack of circulation, the water, generally tranquil, has become warmer and saltier than other parts of the ocean. The currents also tend to trap the sargassum weed in the Sea.

126

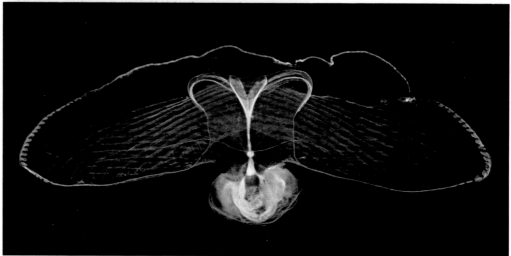

Glittering jewels, planktonic animals drift through the world's ocean in a fantastic array of shapes. At right, a siphonophore extends poison-loaded tentacles that kill prey. A gas-filled float at its top keeps the three-inch-long creature upright. Below, a six-inch-long salp moves through the water by expanding and contracting its barrel-shaped body. Spreading gelatinous wings, a three-inch-wide snail (above) traps minute particles of food. At top, a foraminiferan, an inch-long spiny amoeba, glides some 30 feet below the surface. Such tiny plankton occur by the million, forming one of the primary food sources for animals as large as whales.

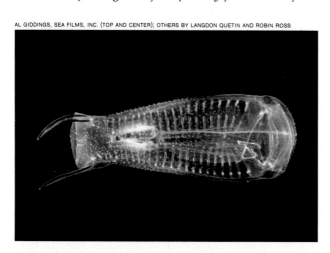

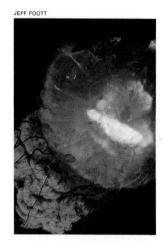

Death trap for some, refuge for others: Adrift in open waters, jellyfish snare and kill small fish, but seem to leave some species alone. Above, a jellyfish with a bell 18 inches in diameter has ingested a fish. Opposite, upper, pompano take refuge among the stinging tentacles of one jellyfish, and medusa fish (opposite, lower) swim undisturbed near another. Marine biologists believe that some fish species have an immunity to the poison, and that others survive among the tentacles through constant alertness and careful movements.

gather in huge numbers to eat them. These fish attract larger ones, until finally the largest predators arrive. At the top of the line in this open-ocean food web are such fish as tuna, swordfish, and sharks.

"When I'm diving in blue water," said Alice, "I spend my time staring at specks of life moving inches an hour or being stared at by large, swift fish with huge teeth." James King, a young man who studies and photographs plankton with Alice, added, "Sharks invariably appear about half an hour after we submerge. Anywhere in the world, that's true. It's a wonder how they know that something's happening, and how they are able to locate us." Part of the answer, I later learned, might be that sharks have special pores in the skin of their heads that sense electromagnetic waves emitted by various creatures.

"One frightening encounter we had with sharks," Jim continued, "was a few days ago when we spotted a great white shark approaching. It circled us once, and we started up toward the boat. We didn't want to tangle with that thousand-pound torpedo of power. As we neared the boat it made a second pass—within just a yard or so of us. I had been told that great whites usually strike on the third pass, so we scrambled onto the boat and pulled our legs up just as that monster zoomed by."

Alice and Jim have come face to face with many of the creatures that inhabit the open sea. "A strange one," Alice said, "is the ocean sunfish, or mola-mola. It's a large disk-like beast that can weigh several hundred pounds. It's extremely gentle, with cow-like eyes, and simply floats near the surface. It exists on a seemingly unsubstantial diet of jellyfish and salps. Once, when I was swimming near a sunfish, it drifted toward me and tried to nibble my swim fin.

"Another time I came across a giant yellow jellyfish drifting just below the surface. It had a pulsating bell that was as big around as a car tire. I banged on it several times, but got no response."

I heard, too, about manta rays, tuna, marlins, and seals. I quickly came to envy Alice and Jim their exciting and varied experiences in the open ocean. As they were talking, I thought of my grandmother, who, at the age of 60, saw the ocean for the first time. A bit overawed by it, she insisted on keeping her distance.

Some of that primal fear of the sea, inspired perhaps by its vastness and unpredictability, still haunts all of us. There are fears of sinking into the salty depths, of being eaten by unknown monsters, of being caught in sudden, violent storms, of becoming lost on an unstable expanse of sameness with no markers except the east-west track of the sun and the pattern of the stars.

Centuries ago people feared different things: sea dragons, great whirlpools, angry sea gods. While such fears have been proved groundless, many others have not.

Not long ago I was in a small boat in the Atlantic Ocean.

A sudden rise in the wind struck the boat viciously, snatching the deck from under my feet. I was shoved backward against hard-edged furniture, and began to feel the first queasy twinges of seasickness. The waves were only three feet high, pushed by a mere 15-mile-an-hour blow. I was thankful that I was not in a hurricane with winds whirling at more than a hundred miles an hour and waves towering to dozens of feet.

Captain Jack Dodd of Harbour Grace, Newfoundland, experienced just such a storm. I talked with him in the kitchen of his small home, which overlooks the gray waters of the North Atlantic. "That blow," he said, "was the worst I've

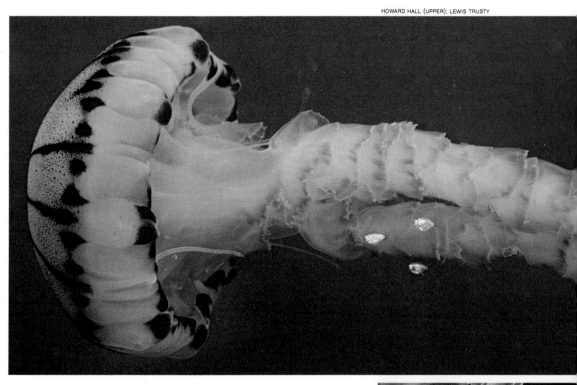

been in during my 28 years of sailing. I was working on a yacht that was sailing from San Diego to Australia. A southeast gale began to push up big rollers. In a few hours the sea had gone mad. Drums of gasoline on the deck broke loose from the moorings and rolled back and forth like wild things, some smashing through the railing. Screaming winds picked up water and threw it right at us, and 60-foot waves crashed over the deck.

"Three big rollers, one right after another, hit the bridge and tore it to pieces. They even twisted steel beams into corkscrews. In the hold, everything and everybody went slamming around. We turned completely about to head into the wind and let the bow split the waves. That eased our bouncing some. Forty-eight hours she blew, with waves like I've never seen before or since—and I've sailed around the world seven times."

131

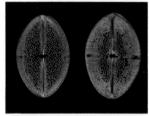

Gemlike diatoms, snowflakes of the sea, float in uncounted billions throughout the world. These tiny plants, here magnified 125 times, form a basic food of the sea.

In Bermuda, a graceful crescent of land some 650 miles off the coast of North Carolina, I asked another experienced sea captain if major storms ever hit the Sargasso Sea, that strange area of doldrums in the middle of the Atlantic Ocean. "Mostly just in the very northern part," Captain David Martin answered as he guided the Bermuda Biological Station's 60-foot research ship from aquamarine shallows to dark-blue deeps. "In the south the Sargasso is a stagnant desert with little wind and rain. That's where the real doldrums, the horse latitudes, are. But even there it can be tricky in summer. The water can get beastly hot—more than 80° F.—and become frenzied if some wind blows in. Waterspouts can drop down from a cloud, forming a whirling column of water from sky to sea."

The Sargasso Sea is the quiet hole in a doughnut-shaped swirl of ocean currents and matching winds. A bowl-shaped shallow sea of extremely warm and salty water, it floats atop the fresher, colder Atlantic depths. The Sargasso Sea is about two-thirds the size of the contiguous United States, and completely surrounds Bermuda, the only land it touches.

Because of the lack of currents and winds, the Sargasso Sea supports a wide variety of life, including drifting seaweed called sargassum. Old sea stories told of sailing ships becoming entangled in these thick growths of weed. They would sit for weeks in the windless heat, trapped in the clutches of the sargassum.

With Captain Martin I sailed into the middle of the Sargasso Sea. All I could see were a few clumps of weed, each no bigger than a pillow, floating past the ship. These small golden bouquets of sargassum are buoyed by gas-filled bladders the size of peppercorns; the plant has no roots. Such small plants, I quickly realized, could not possibly ensnare anything, even if they covered huge areas.

With the help of Captain Martin, I snagged an armful of sargassum with a gaff. To me, it looked like a pile of soggy vegetation devoid of life. But when we shook the plants, out fell a parade of life forms: sea slugs, crabs, shrimp, fishes—none larger than the eraser of a pencil. All were of the same mustard color as the weed.

"Sometimes we find sargassum fish in a bunch of weed," Captain Martin said. "They look exactly like the weed, with trailing leaflike appendages and camouflaging coloration. They're several inches long and seem like monsters compared with these little creatures. They spend their time hiding among the blades of the sargassum, waiting for prey to pass by. Then they strike with incredible speed."

As we examined the pile of sargassum, I noticed several small black balls the size of my thumbnail tucked among the blades. Captain Martin shook his head sadly when I asked about them. "It's tar," he said. "Every armful of weeds will have several balls of it. Oil tankers and other ships wash out their bilges in the open sea, and the circling currents of the North Atlantic concentrate much of it here in the Sargasso. I'm not the only boatman who has noticed that there's less sargassum weed today than just 15 years ago.

"Is there a connection between that and the tar balls? I don't know. But I wonder if some day this will become the sargassumless sea."

A type of alga, this drifting sargassum has been in existence for hundreds of thousands of years. Despite this longevity, it is found in its greatest concentration in the Sargasso Sea. The same currents that create the Sea tend to keep the plant from escaping to other areas of the ocean. But in its

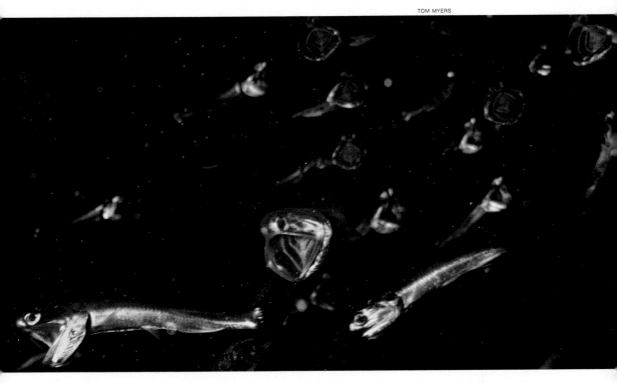

limited environment, sargassum weed shelters and helps feed the young of numerous species—marlin, swordfish, sailfish, tuna, flying fish, green dolphin, and many others.

Larger creatures pass through the Sargasso Sea, but rarely stay for any length of time. "I've seen whales, sharks, and all sorts of big fish," Captain Martin said. "But one of the strangest animals I've ever seen I spotted not far from here a few years ago. It was an oarfish, ten feet long, flat as a knife blade, and with a snakelike head capped by a rooster's coxcomb. Oarfish are probably the inspiration for the old sea-dragon myths. And once you've seen one, it's easy to understand why."

Another sinuous snakelike animal that inhabits the Sargasso Sea for part of its life is the common river eel of North America and Europe. For centuries it was known that young eels appeared in freshwater and coastal areas in the spring

Young herring, anchovy, and smelt strain particles of food from the water with netlike gill rakers in their mouths. These open-water species teem in schools of millions throughout the world's ocean, devouring diatoms and other plankton. In turn these small fishes, several inches long, fall victim to larger predators.

133

Like bombers in formation, dogtooth tuna patrol the Red Sea. Even on the hunt, these three-foot-long predators travel in schools of several dozen. Other members of the tuna family weigh as much as half a ton each, and can swim 70 miles an hour in short bursts. Their fins retract into slots in the body for extra speed. The food web that begins with microscopic plants and tiny drifting animals eventually leads to such large predators as tuna, sharks, and killer whales.

134

and that mature eels left those areas for the open sea in the autumn. However, the genesis of this creature and the steps in its development were puzzles. Aristotle, for instance, believed that "the eels came from what we call the entrails of the earth."

Only within the last few decades has the life cycle of the river eel been at least partly revealed. Hatched at unknown depths in the Sargasso Sea, the young eels soon begin a remarkable migration to either Europe or North America. They wriggle and drift with the currents for three years to reach Europe—one year to reach North America—covering as much as 3,000 miles of open ocean. During the journey they continuously metamorphose, changing from a transparent, leaf-shaped baby, to a ribbonlike fish, to a small eel. Once they reach the coast, the eels, now called elvers, make a further transition. They leave their saltwater environment and swim up freshwater rivers.

There they live for as long as a dozen years, until still other dramatic changes occur. The eels, now about three feet long, lose their characteristic yellow color and turn a glittering silver. Their sex organs mature. Spurred by these changes, the eels leave the freshwater streams by the million and begin their long but unerringly accurate journey back to the Sargasso to spawn—and then to die.

Another creature that may spend part of its life in the Sargasso is the sea turtle. Mature females of the loggerhead, green, and ridley species deposit a clutch of about 120 eggs each on the sandy coasts of the southern United States, Central America, and the Caribbean Islands. Hatchlings—vulnerable babies the size of a half dollar—scramble clumsily to the water. They then drop out of sight.

What happens to these young turtles—where they go, what they eat, how they develop—is still virtually unknown. When the turtles are again observed—after about a year—they have grown measurably, and are about the size of a dinner plate.

Some marine biologists theorize that the baby turtles somehow make their way to the Sargasso Sea, and there feed on the abundant small animals, and possibly on the plants. They remain until they reach a size that will enable them to exist more safely in open waters.

This seemingly empty expanse of doldrums, I was coming to realize as I learned more about the Sargasso, is crucially important to the well-being of many creatures.

Sailing with Captain Martin that day, I also came to appreciate more intimately the perpetual motion of water. Waves and ripples, sometimes large, sometimes small, passed under our boat with regularity. The wind pushed some waves to higher peaks and even swept water into wind-borne fragments of foam. On the horizon in all directions was the same never-ceasing play of wind and water.

I knew that the sea could be put into motion by events other than local weather. Christopher Columbus's sailors,

CARL ROESSLER

Sea dragon of the Pacific, a marine iguana grazes on algae while clinging to submerged rocks off the Galapagos Islands. The two-foot-long reptiles spend most of the day on land, but dive as deep as 35 feet to feed. They can remain underwater for half an hour at a time. A flightless cormorant (opposite), another animal in the Galapagos that has adopted an amphibious life, searches for fishes, octopuses, and crabs. It can dive to depths of 50 feet for as long as ten minutes.

for example, were astonished once when "the sea rose" on a smooth surface with no wind.

Such unexpected disturbances can be caused by tsunami, huge waves produced by underwater earthquakes; by violent storms in other areas of the ocean; or by the moon as it makes the tides. As the moon swings past in its orbit, it creates high tides in waters directly below it and in those on the opposite side of the earth. Halfway in between, troughs, or low tides, are formed.

Other disturbances are caused by the currents that flow through the oceans. In Bermuda some waves spin off from the Gulf Stream, that mammoth surge of warm water that swirls through the North Atlantic.

The Gulf Stream system of currents receives its initial impetus off the Atlantic coast of North Africa, as powerful winds push equatorial waters westward in a stream toward South America. From there they bend north and funnel between Central America and the Caribbean Islands into the Gulf of Mexico. Gently warmed, they gather speed and squeeze between Florida and Cuba, joining with another branch of the system to form the Gulf Stream. They move north along the East Coast at four to six miles an hour, bending slightly eastward off North Carolina and heading toward Europe. Gulf Stream waters, still warm from their trip through the tropics, graze the coasts of Ireland and Scotland, producing palm trees in those cold northern countries. Another branch of the Gulf Stream circles south, returning to its origins off North Africa. A drop of water that made the entire circuit would drift through the North Atlantic for some two and a half years.

Such great sweeping currents flow through every ocean, intermingling water throughout the world. They circulate cold and warm waters and mix nutrients. Currents of wind match the currents of water, and between them much of the world's weather is created. Warm water evaporating into cooler winds, for instance, can produce rain that then sprays a wide area.

One chilly November day, I flew over the Gulf Stream in a single-engine airplane with Hall Watters of Cape Hatteras, North Carolina. On an otherwise clear day, a thick strip of low puffy clouds drifted steadily northward just a few miles offshore.

"They're Gulf Stream clouds," explained Hall, a veteran of 30 years of flying in this area, "and they're drifting right above the main current. I see them whenever the air is cooler than the temperature of the Gulf Stream itself. They usually signify a change in the weather."

As we flew home, I spotted a solitary loggerhead turtle swimming with strong strokes of its flippers eastward in the direction of the Gulf Stream. Many animals, I knew, hitch rides in the fast-moving currents, which are often referred to as the rivers of the sea.

Overleaf: Sea lions plunge into sun-dappled waters off the Galapagos. Padded with blubber for warmth, the mammals weigh as much as 800 pounds. Ferocious bulls rule harems of as many as 30 females, jealously guarding them from other males.

137

Friendly loner, a spotted dolphin romps with Sylvia Earle and then receives a pat (opposite). Dolphins usually travel in schools far out to sea, but this one prefers the company of people, and patrols a 25-mile stretch of shoreline in the Bahamas. Islanders have named it Sandy.

On his voyages of discovery, Columbus made use of the currents in the North Atlantic. Whether or not he had prior knowledge of these streams is unknown, but during his first journey to the New World, he headed south—instead of west—from Spain. Off the coast of North Africa, he caught the current that originates there, and it swept him to an island in the Bahamas that he named San Salvador. On his return voyage, he came upon the Gulf Stream, which carried him eastward toward Europe.

I found another of the great ocean currents in the South Pacific. In contrast to the Gulf Stream, the Peru Current, also called the Humboldt, carries cold waters from the Antarctic region north toward the Equator. I had flown to the Galapagos Islands, a small cluster of volcanoes that straddles the Equator 600 miles west of South America, expecting to find the warmth of the tropics. Instead I discovered that the Peru Current produces a climate there that reminded me of Labrador in early autumn.

It is so cold, in fact, that penguins live on the westernmost islands. They waddle on the volcanic rocks and rocket through the cold seas the way they do in Antarctica.

Hood Island, at the southern end of the group, bears the brunt of the cold, however. Here, the Peru Current mixes with the Cromwell, a cold, deep tongue of water that originates in the mid-Pacific and upwells at the Galapagos. The water temperature in these two currents hovers at about 50° F. The day I explored Hood Island was heavily overcast and marked by a damp chill that penetrated my clothes. I found it hard to believe I was on the Equator.

The same currents that bring cold water and chilly weather to the Galapagos may also have ferried life forms there. Scientists think that most of the animal species and many of the plant species drifted on the Peru Current as it flowed north along the coast of South America, then bent west toward the Galapagos. Sea lions, turtles, seals, penguins, lizards, all originally found their way by swimming or by drifting on logs or on mats of vegetation. Seeds arrived the same way or were carried by birds or borne on the steady trade winds that blow westward across the islands from South America.

Once they were established on the Galapagos, the plant and animal species evolved new forms. Because of the competition for food, one species of lizard partially took to the sea. It evolved into what today is the world's only marine iguana. These two-foot-long reptiles spend most of the day on land. But to feed, they dive into Pacific waters and forage on algae growing on bottom rocks. They can submerge for as long as 30 minutes and go to depths of some 35 feet.

A bird, the flightless cormorant, has given up the air and now also uses the ocean realm to feed. Large, green-eyed birds with shrunken wings, cormorants dive to depths of 50 feet for crabs, octopuses, and small fishes. They can stay underwater for as long as ten minutes. These birds have become so dependent on the sea that they even make their nests of seaweed.

The display of life in the Galapagos region is diverse and bizarre. As Charles Darwin discovered in the mid-1800's, the isolated character of the island group makes a perfect laboratory for the study of adaptation and evolution.

But the Galapagos area is not the only place in the open ocean where the unusual can be found. James King, the young plankton researcher and photographer I met in Santa Barbara, told me of an experience he had during a 24-day excursion in a small sailboat that took him 2,800 miles from San Francisco to Hawaii.

"We were heading west," he said, "and suddenly we came upon a multitude of small jellyfish floating on the surface. They were all moving north, almost as if they were in formation. For two days and nights, over a stretch of 250 miles, we could see nothing but the two-inch-high sails of those jellyfish. There must have been millions of them.

"Another sensational sight I had on that trip occurred one night, when small plants and animals drifting near the surface emitted light. This phenomenon is called bioluminescence, and, with surface creatures, it usually happens when the life forms are disturbed. As the boat moved through the water, there was a trail of glitter following behind. These little glowing dots of light illuminated the waves and even the creatures swimming in them—sharks, porpoises, and once a whole school of squids. It made large jellyfish look like Chinese lanterns."

A new way of observing what happens in the open ocean has just recently been developed by the National Aeronautics and Space Administration. In a far-reaching program sponsored by NASA, a satellite called Seasat-A was launched to monitor the surface of the open sea.

"For the first time," explained project director Don Montgomery, "sensors are gathering data on every bit of the ocean, sweeping large areas repeatedly every several days. The satellite measures currents, tides, temperatures, the speed and direction of winds, the height of waves, and the number of icebergs—among other things. It is like having thousands of ships distributed uniformly across the world's ocean, each taking measurements for a couple of hours many times a week."

But as thorough an observer as this satellite is, it cannot probe beneath the surface. There, underwater scientists like Alice Alldredge must still explore firsthand, floating with the zooplankton to understand their mysteries.

Perhaps it is this combination of technological advance and personal experience that will best help to preserve the open sea and to protect the vast range of species that depends on it. Perhaps it will help safeguard the future generations of offspring spawned by that loggerhead turtle I saw swimming determinedly toward the Gulf Stream.

Underwater ballet: With graceful movements, Sylvia Earle, Sandy the dolphin, and a group of horse-eye jacks glide through aquamarine waters of the Atlantic. When divers enter his domain, Sandy quickly appears, first curiously inspecting them and then wanting to play. "In 25 years of diving," said Sylvia, "meeting Sandy is the peak, the most unusual experience I've ever had."

Sleek blue shark slashes through waters of the Pacific off California, tirelessly scouting the open sea for squids, small fishes, and carrion. This swift and agile predator grows to an average length of 12 feet. In contrast to the streamlined shark, an ocean sunfish, or mola-mola (right), swims sluggishly at the surface of the Pacific. These giants can weigh several hundred pounds, subsisting on a diet of jellyfish. The nearly tailless sunfish sometimes lie on their sides at the surface and allow floating sea gulls to pick parasites from them. A tough covering of leathery skin three inches thick protects them from predators.

146

Female Pacific ridley turtles scramble onto a beach in Costa Rica on a moonlit night. Tens of thousands of ridleys come ashore annually to lay eggs (lower, left) in nests scooped out of the sand with paddlelike flippers. Each turtle will lay about 120 eggs and then return to the sea. Of the hundreds of thousands of eggs deposited each year, only a few hatchlings will survive to maturity. Vulnerable to seabirds, young turtles just out of the shell (below) scuttle toward the water, soon to disappear in the vastness of the open ocean.

THE

Moments before entering the realm of eternal darkness, the submersible Alvin undergoes a final check. In such capsules man has descended into the hostile world of the ocean depths.

NATIONAL GEOGRAPHIC PHOTOGRAPHER EMORY KRISTOF

OCEAN DEPTHS

By Robert D. Ballard

Our tiny submersible pitched and rolled in the long swells of the North Atlantic off the coast of New England. The August sun, a blinding disk high above the horizon, blazed with heat that steadily increased the temperature inside the metal-hulled capsule. As I made final preparations for our descent, I reflected that soon I would trade this sparkling world of light, warmth, and motion for one of total darkness, unremitting cold, and unbelievable pressure.

Within the protective confines of *Alvin*, a research submersible owned by the U. S. Navy and operated by Woods Hole Oceanographic Institution, I was poised more than 12,000 feet above the floor of the Atlantic Ocean. Existing far below, I knew, were life forms both unique and bizarre.

Because of the lack of sunlight, no green plants grow in such ocean depths—the province that contains three-quarters of the world's salt water. Animals live by eating other animals or by snaring decaying waste matter that rains ceaselessly down from the surface. These animals generally are small and strange looking, although some of the fishes reach more than a yard in length. To attract food and to locate one another, many of them emit strange glowing light.

Their world is one of inky blackness, of sparse and scattered life, of overwhelming quiet—and I was eager again to enter it. As a geologist with Woods Hole, I had made many trips to the depths, and each new dive, I had learned, brings its own feelings of excitement and discovery. Along with pilot Larry Shumaker, I was ready to embark on a mission to investigate an extinct volcano in the New England Seamounts, a chain of ancient submarine mountains. We received permission from *Lulu*, our support ship, and cast off the moorings—our last link to the world above the waves.

As we slipped below the surface, I watched a translucent jellyfish drift past the view port, its stinging tentacles dangling down several feet. It was the first living organism in the column of water we would descend through to the bottom. That column, defined by the glow of *Alvin*'s lights, holds a diversity of species, and each individual creature contributes to the nutrients that eventually fall to the bottom. Waste material and the very tissues of the animals and plants when they die all drift downward. It is estimated that at least 30 percent of the ooze making up much of the ocean bottom is skeletal material—the remains of creatures that lived at higher levels.

A whitetip shark, another inhabitant of the column of water, materialized outside the view port, silently scouting *Alvin* for a few moments before swimming away. Sharks, attracted by the unusual noise and behavior of the submersible, often appear as soon as she enters the water. When I see a hammerhead or other potentially dangerous shark, I am always comforted to know that I have several inches of metal surrounding me.

Alvin dropped quickly through the water, and soon

reached a descent rate of a hundred feet per minute. The light outside faded gradually into deeper and deeper blues; the water pressure doubled and then doubled again. Just 15 minutes into the descent, Larry, a tall, light-haired veteran of hundreds of dives, switched on the glowing red cabin lights because the darkness had become absolute.

As we descended I reflected that most of the information and knowledge we have about the deep has been uncovered in the last quarter century or so. Until the early 1900's success in penetrating the ocean depths was measured in a few hundred feet, and little was known about the waters below that. It was once even considered hypothetical that life existed at all at extreme depths.

In the 1930's naturalist William Beebe and engineer Otis Barton designed a steel bathysphere, or diving capsule, with which to penetrate the deep. This bathysphere, winched on a long cable from a support ship, measured just $4\frac{1}{2}$ feet across and weighed two tons. In this "lonely sphere" Beebe and Barton were lowered to a depth of 3,028 feet in 1934 off Bermuda. They thus became the first persons to experience conditions in the ocean depths.

Through a three-inch-thick quartz window, they came face to face with hatchetfish, small fierce-looking creatures, and other animals of the deep. Upon their return, Beebe, fascinated by the adventure, wrote:

"The only other place comparable to these nether regions must surely be naked space itself, far beyond the atmosphere, between the stars, where sunlight has no grip upon the dust and rubbish of planetary air. In the blackness of space, the shining planets, comets, suns, and stars must be closely akin to the world of life as it appears to the eyes of an awed human being in the open ocean half a mile down.

"Ever since the beginnings of history, when man first dared to sail the open sea, thousands upon thousands of human beings had reached these depths. But all these men were dead, drowned victims of war, or tempest and other acts of God.

"We were the first living souls to roam so far in Davy Jones's locker and return."

In little more than a quarter of a century after Beebe and Barton's dive, a bathyscaph named *Trieste* descended ten times farther—to the deepest area in the ocean. On January 23, 1960, Swiss engineer Jacques Piccard and U. S. Navy Lt. Don Walsh steered the *Trieste* 35,800 feet down in the Challenger Deep of the Mariana Trench. Piccard wrote of that dive, "Like a free balloon on a windless day, indifferent to the almost 200,000 tons of water pressing on the cabin from all sides . . . slowly, surely, in the name of science and humanity, the *Trieste* took possession of the abyss, the last extreme on our earth that remained to be conquered."

In the intervening years, diving capsules and submersibles have continued to prove their worth. Indeed, they are essential to the investigation of the deep wilderness. For

Portuguese man-of-war drifts with the tide on a windless day off Florida. Its poisonous tentacles dangle 15 feet deep to snare prey. Such surface dwellers help nurture life all the way to the ocean floor. Their waste matter and even their tissues when they die slowly sink toward the bottom.

here, man cannot dive freely, but instead must rely on machines to transport him.

The red cabin lights in *Alvin* suddenly flickered off, startling me from my thoughts. "I just saw a large shadow pass overhead," Larry called out, "so I thought I'd better turn out the lights."

Peering out of the view port, I saw a swordfish charging at us in the misty glow provided by our outside running lights. The six-foot-long fish came to within inches of the port and then swam back and forth, apparently angered by our intrusion into its domain. Remembering a previous experience with a swordfish, I was glad that Larry had killed the lights in the cabin.

On that occasion, *Alvin* was diving on the Blake Plateau, a submarine terrace off the Carolinas. At about 1,700 feet, a large swordfish attacked the sub, swimming directly at the glowing view port, which it must have assumed was the eye of a giant monster. The pointed sword, $2\frac{1}{2}$ feet long, struck *Alvin* and penetrated a seam. It became wedged in the frame of the sub. The dive was canceled, and *Alvin* brought to the surface for a damage check. Luckily the damages were superficial. But we had learned our lesson: When a swordfish approaches, turn off the lights.

The swordfish outside soon disappeared, but we kept the cabin lights off because we were approaching one of the most fascinating phenomena of the midocean depths—a deep scattering layer. Aboard *Lulu* before our descent, we had seen a cloudlike blur on the sonar that indicated the existence of one of these layers at about 2,000 feet. As we approached that depth, we turned up the outside lights and found ourselves in the midst of thousands upon thousands of small fish darting through the beams.

Early sonar devices often recorded such vast conglomerations of small marine life—sometimes fish, sometimes shrimp, squids, or jellyfish—as solid geological features. The creatures were so densely packed that they reflected, or scattered, the sonar. Several seamounts and other irregularities of the ocean floor that appear on maps based on early sonar readings possibly do not exist—they may have been deep scattering layers that were recorded as something else.

"What in the world do these creatures eat?" Larry asked me. "There's no plant life at this depth because of the lack of sunlight, and there aren't that many other animals that are smaller than they are."

"Some do eat each other," I replied, "but most survive by migrating in a mass toward the surface at night to feed on the more abundant life there. When dawn comes, they drop back into the deep."

Below the deep scattering layer we began to see increasingly large amounts of marine snow—the specks of waste matter that perpetually drift down toward the seafloor.

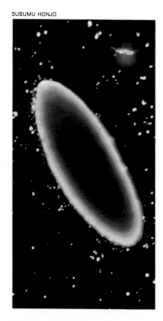

SUSUMU HONJO

Fecal pellet of a tiny drifting animal, magnified 250 times, glows under polarized light. In addition to waste, it contains undigested plant matter. Such pellets raining from above provide an important source of carbon and nitrogen for life in the depths. A pellet may fall for days or even months before reaching the bottom.

These bits of nutrients sometimes take months to reach the bottom, but they are an important ingredient of life in all the ocean depths. As they descend, the particles are attacked by bacteria. The carbon and nitrogen in these particles are vital to the survival of the animals of the deep.

When observed under the powerful magnification of a scanning electron microscope, a particle of marine snow is commonly revealed to be a group of tiny skeletons of organisms that once lived at a higher level in the sea. The skeletons are held together by a mucuslike substance derived from the creature that ate them.

As Larry and I descended deeper through our column

DAVID A. ROSS

of water, we began to encounter more creatures of the deep sea. The animals of the middle depths and the ocean bottom often look like monsters, but many measure only a few inches in length.

Bottom dwellers generally grow slowly and live to older ages than do animals in other parts of the ocean. Some flexible corals, for instance, may take a score or so of years to grow only a couple of inches.

I watched a hatchetfish—one of the creatures Beebe first saw—swim up to the port and gaze in. Magnified, this fish would look as ferocious as a great white shark. Small, needle-sharp teeth line its huge gaping mouth, and bulbous eyes swell from its narrow head. But the hatchetfish is only a couple of inches long.

Much of the fish is mouth, and its lower jaw can open wide enough to take in a meal the same size as itself. Organs along its underside emit light—a feature prevalent among many fishes of the middle depths. Marine biologists theorize that this bioluminescence is a way that animals there attract food, find mates, or frighten predators. Some have

Lantern fish, each about three inches in length, congregate by the million in a huge school some 500 feet thick in the North Atlantic. The school rises toward the surface at night to feed on plankton, then returns to the dark depths by morning. Fish, squids, shrimp, and jellyfish make up such groups, called deep scattering layers for the way they disrupt sonar readings.

153

only a spot or two under the eyes, while others are covered with the glowing organs.

As I watch hatchetfish or other creatures of the deep move past *Alvin*'s view port, I often wonder what it would feel like to be one of them, floating free in the abyss, unencumbered by machines.

I t would be dark, darker than any night on earth. The pressure would be enormous and the cold penetrating. You would drift slowly through the blackness searching for food—perhaps a small fecal pellet dropping from above, or even another animal.

Only occasionally would you sense the presence of a creature—a looming shape, a bright flare of luminescence. But that creature could be anything—a predator, a mate, a meal. You can't tell in the blackness until maybe it's too late. Whatever it is might pass by, and you would continue swimming slowly through the eternal darkness.

"We're nearing bottom," Larry said. "I'm getting an echo on the sonar. We're at a little more than 12,000 feet." As he spoke, he released one of the heavy weights on the side of *Alvin*, and our descent slowed. Soon, in the spray of lights under the submersible, I could see the ocean floor slowly coming closer, seeming to rise toward us, rather than our sinking to it.

Pumping ballast in final adjustments, Larry settled us softly down on the bottom of the Atlantic Ocean—more than two miles below the surface. A cloud of sediment stirred by our landing swirled past the view port and slowly dissipated, pushed by a gentle bottom current running down the slight slope we were on. When the silt had finally settled, I looked out on a typical panorama of a floor in the ocean depths.

In all directions stretched fine bottom sediment, a loose mud composed of marine snow and other materials that have drifted down from the surface for millions of years. Most of the seafloor worldwide is composed of similar materials, but its accumulation is slow—perhaps an inch every thousand years. It is far from being a dead layer, however. In fact, the upper few feet of bottom ooze supports a surprising amount of life.

As I looked through the view port, I saw several purple holothurians, or sea cucumbers, inching along the bottom. These cylindrical creatures vacuum the ocean floor, drawing sediment into their eight-inch-long bodies and gaining nourishment from the nutrients there. They leave long meandering trails in their wakes, redepositing the sediment on the floor.

A red shrimp swam past, its motion through the water more of a crawl than a swimming stroke. These small shrimp are common throughout the deeps, and I have seen them in every area of the ocean where I have submerged. I encounter them so frequently, in fact, that I jokingly tell colleagues that there is one red shrimp that hides aboard *Alvin*. It appears as soon as we reach bottom and swims past the view port for me to see; it then returns to its niche in the submersible and waits for the next trip.

The abundance of these crustaceans illustrates a peculiarity of the depths as compared with other parts of the ocean: their similarity worldwide. In addition to the similarity of environment—depth, temperature, pressure, and lack of light—deeps throughout the ocean have many of the same communities of life populating them. A depth in the Indian Ocean, for instance, may have habitats and organisms comparable to a depth in the North Atlantic. Although

the terrain may differ drastically, a similar sediment composed of like elements blankets the bottom.

Larry and I began to cross the floor of the Atlantic Ocean on our way to explore the soaring undersea mountain that was our goal. We skied across an expanse of soft mud, gradually climbing the slope. Larry called out, "We're coming up on an old paint can. Look! There's a crab living inside it. If it weren't for that paint can, I'll bet the crab wouldn't last very long."

A few moments later we came upon a piece of wood riddled by boring animals. Probably jettisoned from a boat, the wood provided a hiding place and food for the borers. These animals are opportunistic creatures that grow and multiply rapidly when sustenance suddenly presents itself in a realm generally short of food.

Like a starburst, a Porpita *nearly two inches wide floats on the surface, feeding by sweeping the water with stinging tentacles. Overleaf: A sargassum crab hitches a ride on a salp chain. Shifting surface currents will break the chain apart within a few days. Any dead salps will sink toward the bottom.*

(Continued on page 160)   155

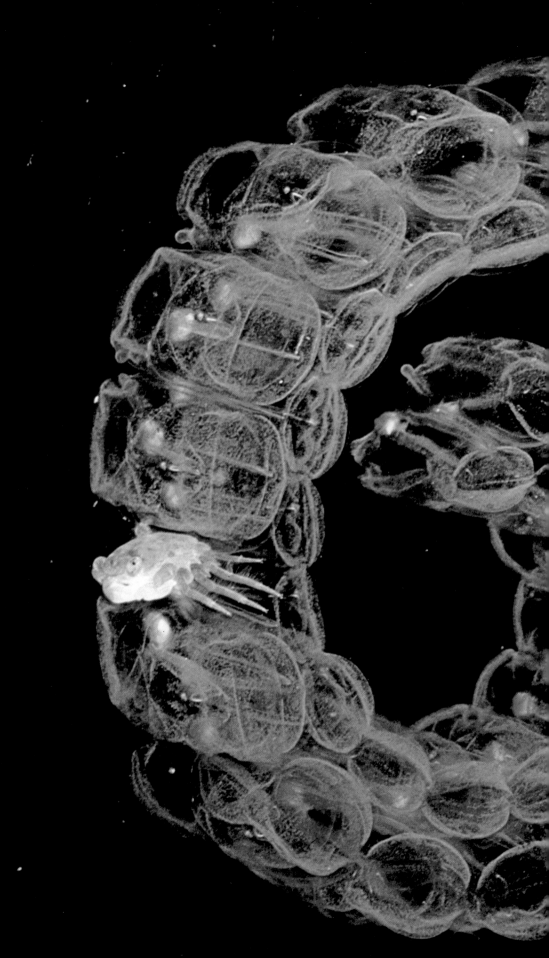

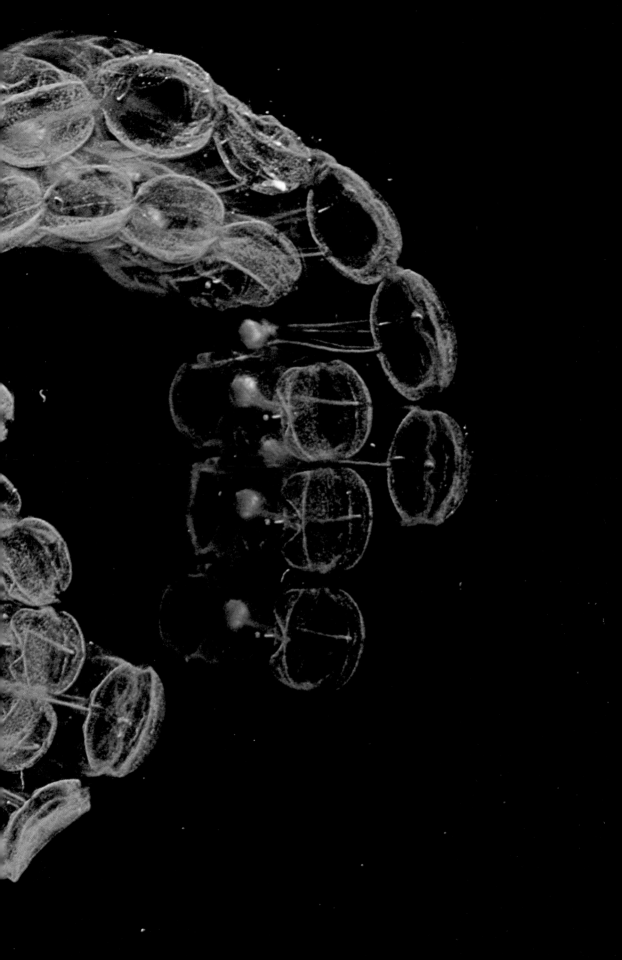

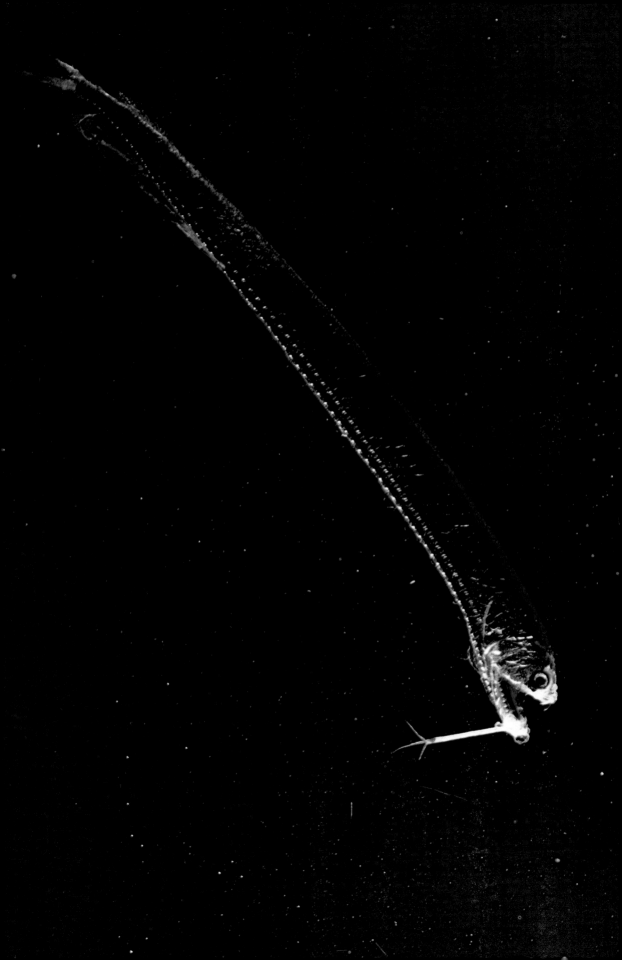

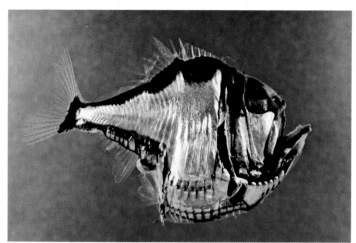

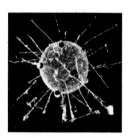

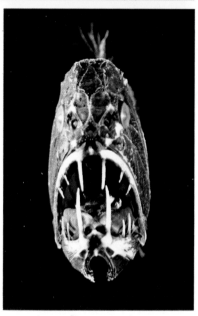

Fearsome in appearance, many deep-sea creatures rarely grow longer than a foot. Scarce food and harsh conditions characterize their habitat. A 12-inch-long Stomias (opposite) extends a luminescent lure from its lower jaw. Many creatures of the deep emit light, possibly to draw food, to attract mates, or to frighten predators. A two-inch-long hatchetfish (top, right) has bulging tubular eyes that look for prey swimming above. The cavernous mouth of a four-inch fangtooth (right) can hold a fish as large as itself. Its ability to swallow so much proves important in the desolate deep. An eight-inch-long cat shark (below) lives near the bottom of the Pacific. A radiolarian colony (above) has a skeleton of silica, a glasslike component of ocean-bottom ooze.

LANGDON QUETIN AND ROBIN ROSS (FANGTOOTH); L.P. MADIN (RADIOLARIAN); OTHERS BY BRUCE H. ROBISON

However, these man-made objects are alien to the ocean depths and present ecological problems. Even the single paint can, innocuous as it may seem, may introduce something potentially unsettling to the wilderness balance of the deep. Recently, the amount of waste, wreckage, and garbage found on the seafloor has dramatically increased. And dumping of such materials as radioactive waste in the deepest trenches may work to the detriment of mankind. As food, fuel, and mineral resources on land and in the shallows continue to be depleted, man may one day turn to the deep to find the things he needs for his own survival. If this realm has been used as a dump, he may have destroyed a vital habitat as well as thrown away resources for generations to come. Because of the slow-changing conditions of the deep, great care must be taken not to disturb this fragile zone of life.

I once received dramatic proof of the slow recycling rate of the ocean depths when some colleagues with whom I was working came across a World War II fighter plane while diving in *Alvin* a mile down off New England. They were cruising the muddy bottom when the familiar shape of a plane came into sight.

It was eerily intact, they said, as if someone had flown it in, taxied to a stop, and then parked it. They half expected to see the pilot clambering down from the cockpit. The plane was in good condition, relatively untouched by its years in this world of darkness, cold, and pressure. They jotted down its registration number. Later, after a little homework, we discovered that the plane had come from an aircraft carrier based in Rhode Island shortly after World War II. Somehow it had fallen off the craft and glided to the bottom, more than a mile down.

I had another firsthand experience with the lack of decomposition at depth when *Alvin* slipped her moorings on the surface several years ago and sank more than 5,000 feet. The crew was just climbing aboard *Alvin* for a mission when the cables holding her to *Lulu* parted. She dropped into the ocean and began taking water through the open hatch. The crew miraculously escaped as *Alvin* filled with water and plummeted to the bottom.

After ten months of sporadic searching, we found *Alvin*. She was sitting right side up in the mud and appeared to have only minor damage. Using *Aluminaut*, another submersible, and the Navy ship *Mizar*, we towed *Alvin* to the surface and then transferred her to Woods Hole for cleaning and maintenance. We were amazed to find that little damage had occurred and that the crew's lunch of apples and bologna sandwiches was intact and still edible! If *Alvin* had sunk in a shallow ecosystem like a coral reef, she would have been encrusted with corals, sponges, and barnacles. Fishes would have made their homes inside her, and some hungry creature would have found and devoured the lunch.

Larry and I were now just beginning to climb the steep

slope of our undersea mountain. We passed a jumble of large, round boulders that seemed completely out of place. Larry asked how they got there.

"They're glacial erratics," I explained. "During the last Ice Age—some 12,000 years ago—huge glaciers bulldozed the land, scouring the earth and picking up rocks and other debris. The powerful grinding action of the glaciers gradually smoothed and rounded the rocks, and carried them eventually to the sea. There, great icebergs broke off from the glaciers—just as they do now in Greenland and Antarctica—and drifted on the surface. Eventually they melted and dropped their load of boulders. The rocks we see here may have come from various parts of North America that were covered with ice.

"In fact, many of the sediments found in the deep have their origins in different areas of the world. For instance, sand from the Sahara, blown high into the atmosphere by raging winds, eventually settles onto the ocean. It then gradually drifts to the bottom.

"Volcanoes hurl great volumes of dust, ash, and glass into the air. High-level wind currents sometimes circulate them worldwide, and they gradually sift down to earth. Since the ocean covers seven-tenths of the globe, it receives most of the fallout. Eventually this volcanic material adds to the layer of mud on the bottom."

Volcanoes also affect the deep in much more dramatic ways. Undersea mountain ranges, built by churning forces within the earth, rear thousands of feet from the seafloor in certain areas. In other places narrow trenches plunge to great depths. Within the last dozen years, these great topographic features have been knitted together by a far-ranging theory that explains the present configuration of the earth—the theory of plate tectonics.

According to this theory, the earth's crust is broken into huge slabs that drift on what may be great circulating currents far below the surface. The slabs, called plates, are splitting apart in some areas and colliding in others, creating earthquakes and volcanoes.

Where two plates separate, a tear in the earth is produced. Through this tear rises magma, or molten material; some of it spills out on the ocean floor as lava and hardens. As the plates continue to spread, magma also continues to flow upward, forming more rock. This rock, fractured and uplifted, eventually builds into great submarine mountain ranges. The Mid-Atlantic Ridge—a 12,000-mile-long mountain chain in the Atlantic Ocean—was built, and is continuing to be built, in this way. It soars more than 20,000 feet in some places, breaking the surface occasionally to form such dots of land as Iceland and the Azores.

Where two plates collide, trenches are formed as one plate slips below the other. The interaction between the two produces shattering earthquakes and towering volcanoes.

Walking on jointed legs, a six-inch-long crab (above) crosses a mound of limestone 2,000 feet down off the Bahamas. Nearby, a fish (opposite, upper) slips among branches of a coral. Retractable tentacles of mud anemones snare food 800 feet down off New England. Many bottom dwellers grow slowly. These anemones, perhaps 20 to 50 years old, stand only 20 inches high.

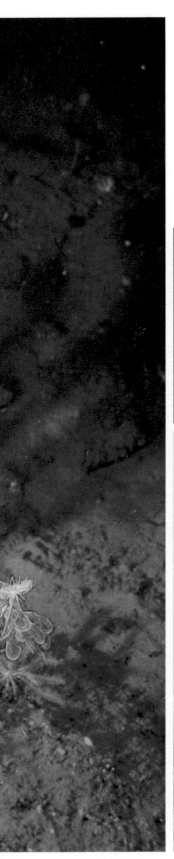

Spidery lobsters scuttle across black coral 1,300 feet below the surface off California. Such coral growths on the usually silty ocean floor provide anchorages for feather stars and sponges. In the Galapagos Rift, warm water flows from seafloor vents, supporting small oases of life (bottom). Crabs climb among 18-inch-long tube worms attached to the volcanic rock a mile and a half down. At the bottom of the Caribbean, a tulip-shaped sponge (lower, right) clings to a rock, filtering nutrients that drift down from above. A sablefish (below) prowls the depths; as juveniles, these fish live near the surface.

*Manganese nodules, some
as big as baseballs, speckle
an area of Pacific seafloor
(upper). These deposits
generally form around
rocks or shells. Scientists
look to such formations
as a future source of
manganese, copper, nickel,
and cobalt. A sea star
(lower) inches past small
sponges along a geological
fault in the Caribbean.
Bottom sediments edge
against the vertical rock.*

Through such a process, the Andes of South America continue to grow.

The comprehensive, global concept of plate tectonics is constantly being refined because of recent investigations into the ocean depths. The advent of submersibles such as *Alvin* permitted earth scientists to explore regions that are tectonically active. In a project called FAMOUS, scientists from several countries used three submersibles to study the Mid-Atlantic Ridge.

Larry and I took part in that wide-ranging project and made many dives together to active areas. We saw young volcanoes rising from the blackness of the ocean bottom, lava flows stretching along the seafloor, deep fissures cleaving the rock.

I was amazed at the different shapes the lava took as it was extruded onto the ocean bottom. Instead of forming easy-flowing rivers of lava as it often does on land, the molten material comes out of the earth like toothpaste being squeezed from a tube. When the magma, heated to about 2,200° F., comes in contact with the frigid waters of the deep, it quickly cools, forming bulbous mounds called pillows. The cooled crust of these pillows insulates the lava within, allowing it to flow across the seafloor. When the lava first meets the water, the top layers cool so quickly that they form an obsidian-like black glass.

Another series of dives took us 220 miles off the Galapagos Islands, a group of volcanoes rising 20,000 feet from the floor of the Pacific. During those dives we explored another rift in the ocean floor that allows lava to escape from the earth. But we found more than lava; from several cracks in the rock, water was also pouring out. It was heated, and it shimmered as it mixed with the colder seawater. This outpouring apparently originates with seawater that seeps into the volcanic rock, becomes warmed at depth, and then circulates back up through fissures.

To me, the most amazing quality of this water is not that it exists, but that it supports—in the midst of the inhospitable ocean depths—an unexpectedly dense and unusual circle of life. Near the springs, large clams several inches across open and close their shells; crabs crawl among the waving bodies of giant tube worms; fishes and octopuses flit past above them.

And yet, this whole spectrum of life exists without the benefit of green plants, which provide the initial impetus for life in other ecosystems. Here, specialized bacteria perform the work of green plants, chemically interacting with elements in the sea and with hydrogen sulfide suspended in the volcanic water. These bacteria, combined with the life-encouraging warmth of the water itself, support a unique food web.

Larry and I were now nearing the top of the volcano we had been climbing. Its flanks were composed of lava probably tens of millions of years old—a striking contrast to the fresh pillow lavas I had seen along the Mid-Atlantic Ridge and off the Galapagos.

As we climbed, we passed rock walls brightly colored with yellow sponges and red anemones. Pinkish brittle stars—relatives of sea stars—scuttled among the rocks, which were colored a deep black. This black is actually a residue of manganese that coats the rocks—a kind of marine rust that precipitates from the seawater. Also rich in copper, cobalt, and nickel, these deposits are a resource of the future; several nations have already investigated the possibilities of mining them.

At the top of the volcano, Larry spotted a massive outcrop that was covered with manganese. Using *Alvin*'s mechanical arm, he reached over and rubbed off the black coating, revealing a light-colored substance that turned out to be stony coral. I speculated on what must have happened for this coral—a shallow-water species—to be here, 7,000 feet down.

At some point, this volcano was much closer to the surface; perhaps 150 million years ago the Atlantic was considerably shallower than it is now. Coral reefs could therefore flourish at the top of the mountain just as they do today around such volcanic islands as Martinique in the Caribbean. When the volcanic activity slowed and the Atlantic deepened, however, the volcano began to subside. For a while, the coral probably kept pace with the sinking, but finally the volcano subsided to a level where sunlight no longer stimulated the coral growth, and so it died out.

We had now reached the topmost pinnacle of the mountain, and we decided to return to the surface. The underwater telephone crackled as Larry reported our intention to *Lulu*. He detached a couple of 250-pound weights from the sides of *Alvin*, and we began to rise. Quickly, the rumpled top of the volcano receded, and soon we were surrounded again by black water.

As we ascended I realized how cold and cramped I had become in the submersible, and I suddenly longed for the warmth and brightness of the clear New England afternoon above. Slowly, imperceptibly, black yielded to blue as we left the realm of the deep.

I reflected on what mankind has learned of that nether region in the last 25 years; our knowledge has probably increased at least a hundredfold during that time. And that knowledge has led us to new understandings not only of the ocean depths but also of the complex workings of our entire globe. The deep, we have discovered, is not isolated from the rest of the earth, but rather is an integral component of it, related to every part of the ocean, and to the land and atmosphere as well.

As *Alvin* broke surface and sunlight streamed into the cabin, I wondered what we would discover in the ocean depths in the next 25 years.

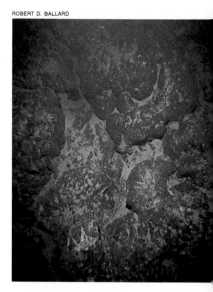

Bulbous pillow lavas off the Galapagos form as molten matter encounters the frigid press of waters in the deep. Lava hardens into mounds, its outer layer cooling quickly into glass. Overleaf: Ten thousand feet down in the Caribbean, Alvin *crosses the silt-covered floor of the Cayman Trough—like all ocean depths, a world of inky blackness, icy cold, and immense pressure.*

THE

*Hurtling skyward, a 30-foot-long humpback whale breaches
in frigid waters off Alaska. Earth's polar seas—harsh in climate
but rich in nutrients—sustain surprising numbers of creatures.*

POLAR SEAS

By Joseph B. MacInnis

Translucent plates of ice glittered above my head with an eerie brilliance. A huge rampart of white loomed before me, plunging deep into violet waters and gradually disappearing into purple nothingness far below. I shivered, took a long, slow breath, and fully savored the moment.

I was swimming directly beneath the North Pole, the top of the world, the empty realm on the map where all meridians meet and every direction is south. It is a magical place where the summer sun never sets and where winter brings six months of darkness.

Suspended in the frigid waters, I traced the jagged outline of the ice wall in front of me. Unlike the thin surface ice overhead, this wall was thick, dense, and deep. Called a pressure ridge, this colossal structure was created by the slow but inexorable collision of two giant ice floes.

Pushed by mighty forces of wind and current, the edges of the floes crashed together and were fractured into blocks taller than a man and wider than a football field. These blocks gradually built a house-high ridge above the surface of the ice. But like an iceberg, the tortured bulk remained mostly underwater. Directly in front of me, thousands of tons of shattered ice were interlocked into the keel of a pressure ridge. The bottom of the keel was tilted obliquely and vanished far below.

The ice-cold water beneath the North Pole was so astonishingly clear that it seemed like air. Through this water, free of sediment, wave action, and organic growth, I could see the details of another jumbled pressure ridge more than 300 feet away.

Below me the floor of the Arctic Ocean dropped away for almost three miles. At the bottom, I knew, was the Polar Abyssal Plain, an expansive basin that was abutted by the Lomonosov Ridge. This 10,000-foot-high range of submerged, flat-topped mountains runs in an almost straight line for more than a thousand miles across the bottom of the Arctic Ocean. It links the continental shelf north of Canada's Ellesmere Island with the shelf off the Soviet Union's New Siberian Islands. These great topographic features at the bottom of the Arctic Ocean, like millions of miles of the sea itself, have never been seen by human eyes—they have only been detected by sonar.

The waters of earth's two polar seas are the most remote and the least understood in all the ocean realm. Protected by distance and darkness, by wind and cold, their physical and biological processes are hidden beneath thick layers of brawling ice. The polar oceans lie at the ends of the earth—both geographically and scientifically—and remain even today relatively unexplored. Only within the last two decades have scientists been able to submerge in the polar seas, diving deep and staying for significant periods of time.

These two regions, the Arctic and the Antarctic, are separated by thousands of miles. They are strikingly similar in some ways and intriguingly different in others. At the top of the globe is the hollow of the Arctic basin, 5.1 million square miles of frozen ocean surrounded by land. At the bottom of the globe is the hump of Antarctica, 5.5 million square miles of frozen land surrounded by ocean. The shape of the Arctic Ocean is roughly similar to that of the Antarctic continent, and the deepest depth of the Arctic—about 17,000 feet— nearly matches the greatest height of the Antarctic—the Vinson Massif at 16,860 feet.

The Arctic Ocean is ringed by Canada, the United States, the Soviet Union, Norway, and Greenland. Antarctic waters, in effect, are simply the southernmost reaches of the Atlantic, Pacific, and Indian oceans.

The dominant feature of both polar seas, of course, is water. But here, unlike any other place on earth, it is evident throughout the year in all of its states: liquid, ice, and vapor. Of the three, it is the ice—sprawling in huge white plates in all directions to the horizon—that most staggers the imagination. It is gracefully shaped and diamondlike in its beauty. But the ice is also hard, cold, and unforgiving.

Diving beneath pack ice, particularly when it is in motion during spring thaw, can prove extremely risky. A few years ago I was on an expedition off Newfoundland to film harp seals under late-winter pack ice that creaked and groaned as it moved.

I submerged through a narrow fissure in the ice and soon became so enthralled with my work that I failed to notice that the crack was closing. Fortunately, I was suspended from a nylon rope gripped by two strong Newfoundlanders. They whisked me out of the water like a hooked fish just as the fissure slammed shut. "You was lucky, me boy," one of them said with a shake of his head. "A few more seconds and she would have nipped you good."

The formation of sea ice is a dramatic process in which temperature, wind, and ocean current all play major roles. If the surface is calm and the temperature suddenly drops, for instance, ice that is highway-smooth can form on the sea for miles in all directions. Eskimos have told me of stretches of water that were navigable in the morning but frozen solid enough to walk on by afternoon.

After sea ice is formed, the wind and ocean currents begin to bully it. The smooth surface is broken into thousands of small ice floes that bump together and rub against each other. The irregular floes are thus rounded, and have the appropriate name of pancake ice.

When the wind quiets, new ice begins to form between the pancakes, locking them together into a rough, craggy surface. More ice freezes onto the underwater surfaces of the pancakes—quickly at first, and then more slowly as the ice becomes thicker. Within days, and sometimes within hours, the liquid ocean has become the solid non-land of the polar regions.

To divers who swim below it *(Continued on page 176)*

JOSEPH B. MACINNIS

Plunging ramparts of ice, thick pressure ridges confront a diver exploring the Arctic Ocean beneath the North Pole. A thin frozen layer coats the surface.

Huge mouth agape, a humpback whale off Alaska scoops up thousands of krill—small shrimplike crustaceans (below). To trap the krill, the whale quickly swims in a circle underwater, exhaling air as it moves. The rising air bubbles form a barrier that momentarily corrals the fast-moving krill. The whale then rises through the center of the circle with its mouth open, straining the crustaceans from the seawater with baleen, bonelike plates in its mouth. Vast numbers of krill live in both the Arctic and Antarctic, providing a major source of food to larger animals—fishes, seals, penguins, seabirds, and baleen whales.

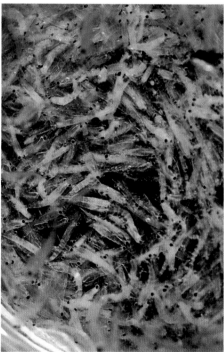

BOTH BY AL GIDDINGS, SEA FILMS, INC.

173

Shaggy polar bear leaps between ice floes
drifting in summer on the Arctic Ocean.
The largest surface predators in the Arctic,
polar bears stalk seals in the water or as they
sun on pack ice. One blow of a bear's huge
paw can crush a seal's head. During the
cold, dark Arctic winter, the thousand-
pound bears wait near holes in the ice to
catch seals as they surface to breathe.

Craning its neck, a polar bear searches for seals in cold Arctic waters. A skillful swimmer,
the polar bear uses its forepaws as paddles and the broad back paws as a rudder.
A thick layer of fat and two kinds of fur—a dense, soft undercoat covered by long,
oily outer hair—insulate the bear from the cold of both the water and the severe
winters. Bears wander almost constantly during the summer months, loping along the
surface of the pack ice or swimming between floes. In pursuit of prey they run in
a lumbering gallop at 25 miles an hour over short distances. Once threatened
with extinction, polar bears today have a stable population of about 20,000 animals.

*Head thrown back,
proboscis inflated, a bull
elephant seal trumpets
noisily. Bulls expand their
snouts when threatened or
when defending their
harems. Largest of all the
seals, the bulls weigh as
much as three tons and
reach lengths of 20 feet.*

and to captains who pilot ships through it, polar ice can be an awesome adversary. Over the years scientists and mariners have developed a specialized vocabulary to describe its many forms and its behavior. Fresh ice is known as frazzle or grease. There is young ice, first-year ice, and old ice. When it is melting, ice is called brash or rotten. Pack ice can be rafted, hummocked, or ridged.

Several summers ago I was in a small wooden boat crossing Cumberland Sound in Canada's eastern Arctic. Near midnight we were stopped by shifting pack ice that suddenly surrounded the boat. From the deck I could hear the muted grinding noise of ice meeting the hull. I closed my eyes and pictured a sharp edge of ice stabbing through the planking of the boat with the ease of scissors cutting paper. I had heard many stories of ships being slowly crushed to splinters by encroaching pack ice. I envisioned the remains of our small boat—a few random planks—scattered across the top of the ice.

We waited tensely for several hours, expecting at any moment to be left stranded with a destroyed boat. But somehow, mysteriously, the pressure lessened, the ice receded, and we were able to continue.

Of all the forms of polar ice, to me the most impressive is the iceberg. These floating white islands, which sometimes weigh a million tons, break off from the great glaciers of the Arctic and the Antarctic. In the Northern Hemisphere, some 20,000 icebergs are calved each year, and 90 percent of these come from glaciers on the west coast of Greenland. Some Arctic icebergs are more than half a mile long and reach a hundred feet into the air. A record height reported was a dizzying 550 feet above sea level—almost as tall as the Washington Monument.

Each year about 375 icebergs drift south from Greenland on the Labrador Current and reach the Grand Banks of Newfoundland. From a distance icebergs look like graceful marble cliffs or floating castles of alabaster. Smoothed by wind, wave, and the heat of the sun during their four-year journeys, they do not seem threatening. However, large spurs of ice projecting underwater create unseen hazards for ships. In 1912, when the *Titanic* struck an iceberg, a large, hard-edged spur ripped a 300-foot-long gash in the ship's side. More than 1,500 people drowned when the "unsinkable" *Titanic* went down.

One summer, I dived down the flank of a huge berg that was stranded in the shallows off Baffin Island. The afternoon sun burned low on the horizon. The iceberg, mountainous in its majesty, caught the sun's light, casting a long dark shadow.

I quickly submerged and discovered a ledge of thin ice hanging from the berg. The dying rays of the sun, refracted through this ledge, colored the ice a strange shade of blue. It was not the blue of the sea or the sky, but a blue that glowed as if lit by some otherworldly fire.

With a gentle exhalation I eased into the water along the sheer face of the berg. Even through my thick neoprene gloves the ice felt hard as stone. But unaccountably its surface was blurred, like the wavery lines that quiver above a road on a hot summer day. I thought my eyes, stung by the cold, were playing tricks on me.

Then I realized that I was seeing the zone where fresh water, melting from the top of the iceberg and coursing down its sides, mixed with the salt water of the sea. Being of different densities, the two liquids mingled unevenly where they first came into contact. I dropped down a few feet and my vision quickly cleared.

The great bulk of the iceberg fell away below me like a long, bleached hill. As I descended to 50 feet, its contour changed into a series of pitched terraces, each one, I thought, a perfect slope for downhill skiing. At 100 feet I stopped. The ice stretched far below the pale wash of my flashlight with no evidence of ending. I could continue exploring its slopes and crevices for an eternity, it seemed.

As large as this iceberg appeared, however, it was minuscule compared to some of the monsters that are spawned in Antarctica. Many of the biggest ones there originate from the Ross Ice Shelf, a huge plateau that covers 200,000 square miles—an area about the size of Texas. The slowly moving ice, most of it floating on the Ross Sea, varies in thickness from 2,300 feet at its junction with the land to about 300 feet at the seaward edge.

In 1841 Sir James Clark Ross sailed two small, double-hulled vessels, *Erebus* and *Terror*, through dense pack ice and into the frozen sea later named for him. There he confronted an immense barrier of ice. Before him lay white, splintered cliffs, 150 to 200 feet high, that extended for more than 500 miles. "It is impossible to conceive a more solid-looking mass of ice," recorded the stolid admiral in his ship's log for January 28. "Not the smallest appearance of any rent or fissure could we discover throughout its whole extent, and the intensely bright sky beyond it but too plainly indicated the great distance to which it reached to the southward. Many small fragments lay at the foot of the cliffs, broken away by the force of the waves, which dashed their spray high up the face of them."

For days Ross guided his tiny ships along the high, unbroken wall, but was unable to find a passage through. He wrote, ". . . we might with equal chance of success try to sail through the Cliffs of Dover as penetrate such a mass."

The Ross Ice Shelf, although the largest, is only one of many sheets that slope into the sea and produce icebergs. It is not surprising that southern icebergs are so large, for they are calved from the greatest expanse of ice in the world. Antarctica is covered by nearly 95 percent of the snow and ice on the planet. If it all melted, the level of the world's ocean would rise some 180 feet.

Icebergs calved from these huge shelves have unbelievable dimensions. The seaward edges of the shelves are perpetually breaking off and producing long, flat-topped bergs. Some are 45 miles long and have an area larger than Rhode Island. Over a period of months, they drift north on ocean currents, slowly diminishing in the increasing warmth of the sun.

By itself the ice at both poles is virtually incompatible with life—it is a frozen desert. But in the surrounding water, life abounds. The frigid waters of the Antarctic, in fact, support more individual animals and plants per cubic mile than the systems in more temperate climates. The southern

Tusked giants, Pacific bull walruses pack together on an ice floe off Alaska. Walruses hook their tusks on the ice to help them clamber out of the water. The marine mammals also use the two-foot-long tusks for defense. Walruses can remain submerged for about ten minutes while diving for clams and other invertebrates. Protected from the icy water by blubber and a thick, leathery hide, bull walruses weigh as much as 4,000 pounds.

ocean is one of the richest communities of life on the planet. But it has a boundary—the Antarctic Convergence, a 10,000-mile-long front that circles the continent.

At the point of the convergence, two different kinds of oceanic waters meet and mix. The colder, less salty water from Antarctica sinks below the warmer water coming from the tropics. The convergence lies entirely outside the Antarctic Circle, its latitude varying with currents, winds, and seafloor contours. Generally, it is about 2,500 miles from the South Pole.

Crossing the Antarctic Convergence on a southbound ship brings immediate changes. The air temperature suddenly drops, the climate becomes more severe, and the life forms seen on nearby islands have obviously adapted to the harsh weather.

The greatest transformation takes place in the sea, however, well hidden from human eyes. The water temperature drops several degrees, and in the black fathoms under the ship there is a constant upwelling of bottom water, rich in oxygen and minerals. Here, in this rich water, is the kingdom of the krill.

Small shrimplike crustaceans about two inches long,

krill are vital organisms in the food web of the Antarctic. They are the main food of fishes, seals, penguins, seabirds, and the great baleen whales, which scoop them from the water by the million. These small crustaceans swim in schools so vast and so dense that they can be detected by remote sensing satellites. It is estimated that between 800 million and 5 billion tons of krill exist in Antarctic waters.

It was once believed that the frigid climate and the lack of sunlight would inhibit growth in the Antarctic. However, a more important factor to the support of life is the constant supply of nutrients carried toward the surface by upwelling currents. This so-called vertical instability of the water cre-

ates conditions that nurture a food web ranging from tiny diatoms to blue whales, earth's largest creatures.

In contrast the Arctic Ocean is much less productive. "It is clear that the Arctic Ocean as a whole is vertically very stable at all times of the year," writes Dr. Max Dunbar, a Canadian biologist who has studied the waters of the north for 40 years. "Since light and temperature are not likely to be limiting the annual production, the low productivity of the Arctic Ocean must reasonably be put down to this stability." Because fewer nutrients are stirred from the bottom, fewer animals live in the Arctic.

Since 1970 I have explored more than 25 cold-water sites in North America. I have dived during all seasons of the year—when the summer sun blazed for 24 straight hours and when winter temperatures plummeted to 50 degrees below zero. At almost every location, I discovered that life was scarce; the creatures I did see were generally small and colorless. Compared with the waters of a coral reef in the tropics, Arctic waters seem barren.

There were some notable exceptions, however. One August day, near Clearwater Fiord on Baffin Island, I dived into a shallow river that seemed to tremble with the life it

Mellow brown eyes guide a torpedo-shaped harp seal through the murky world beneath Arctic ice. In the water killer whales and sharks pursue the 400-pound seals; on the ice the mammals fear only polar bears—and man. Furriers desire the seal's thick pelt for coats and other garments. But they particularly seek infant pups, like the one above, for their soft, snowy pelts. An international agreement limits the killing of harp seals and their pups.

181

Patches of green in a world of white, small kelp plants grow on the floor of the Arctic Ocean. The tenacious plants survive at depths of as much as 300 feet despite the cold and the lack of sunlight. As if for warmth, a tiny snailfish curls on a blade of kelp.

held. The river, which emptied into a large saltwater bay, was packed with arctic char, hundreds of sleek torpedoes heading upstream.

One of the dominant fish species of the Arctic coast, the char is related to the salmon and measures two feet long. Red-fleshed and fat, the fish often weigh 18 pounds. The char I swam with, glittering above the rocks in front of me, were heading back to a distant lake to spawn after spending several weeks feeding in the sea. They were swimming rapidly, struggling against the strong current, trying to return home before the freeze-up.

On another occasion I joined an expedition searching for bowhead whales in the Chukchi Sea off northern Alaska. During several dives below the ice, my colleague Rick Mason and I swam through gossamer curtains formed by millions of microscopic plants and animals. Even the under-surface of the ice was spotted with webs of muted greens and yellows. Polar waters are usually crystal clear with excellent visibility, but Rick and I lost sight of each other when we were only ten feet apart. "It was like swimming through a dust storm," said Rick. "I've never seen so many living things in one place at one time."

The reason for the unexpected profusion of life was that the plankton were blooming. When winter releases its frozen grip, and the ice begins to crack, the nurturing rays of the sun penetrate the water, causing explosions of microscopic life. Suddenly, the clear water becomes cloudy and green as phytoplankton, tiny floating plants, begin to multiply. These simple plants form the basic unit of food in both the Arctic and Antarctic. Krill and similar species of small animals feed on the phytoplankton, and, in turn, become food for higher life forms such as marine mammals.

The most conspicuous members of polar wildlife, marine mammals—whales, walruses, seals—are specifically adapted for life in the cold oceans. They have short, heat-conserving limbs that serve as paddles for both steering and propulsion. They maneuver easily around and under the ice, finding breathing holes where none seem to exist. For survival in their constantly frigid world, polar marine mammals have abundant insulation—large quantities of fat, muscle, and fur.

The largest of these animals, whales, elephant seals, and walruses, usually have some hair and a tough leathery hide. Under this hide is a thick layer of fat, which not only provides warmth but also is an important source of energy when food supplies run low.

Generally, seals are smaller than most other marine mammals. But they are also more graceful, agile, and lively in the water. On several dives I have watched with delight their fluid movements—the arch of the back, the swish of flippers, the soaring vertical flight. Unlike fishes and whales, which tend to stay horizontal, seals twist, dive, and spin in all directions with constant, playful ease.

The fur seal, covered with a thick, lustrous pelt, lives along the subpolar edges of both cold seas. The Alaska fur seal of the Bering Sea was hunted nearly to extinction for this pelt. Protected by international law since 1911, the fur seal has increased its population. Today, there are more than two million of them.

The fur seals of the south polar regions once densely inhabited the islands and waters surrounding the continent. This area was then the richest fur seal breeding ground in the world.

Fur hunters began decimating the population of seals soon after Captain James Cook set foot on South Georgia Island in 1775. On January 17 of that year Cook recorded in his diary, "I landed in three different places, displayed our Colours and took possession of the Country in his Majestys name. . . . Seals . . . were pretty numerous . . . perhaps the most of those we saw were females for the Shore swarm'd with young cubs."

O nly forty years after Cook, the principal breeding areas of the southern fur seal—the South Shetland Islands—were discovered. In 1821-22 more than 300,000 animals were killed there. Within eight years the herds of the South Shetland Islands were eliminated. Other nearby islands—Marion, Kerguélen, Macquarie, and the South Orkneys—were systematically plundered and every fur seal killed.

The most profitable market for sealskins at that time was Canton, where a Chinese merchant had developed a technique for removing the coarse outer hairs of a pelt while leaving the soft undercoat. The pelts were then made into fur coats or used to insulate the walls and floors of buildings. To supply this insatiable market, nearly every fur seal in the Antarctic was hunted down.

In the 1930's the British research ship *Discovery* visited one of the few surviving rookeries, on Bird Island near South Georgia. Only 12 pups could be counted in a population of one hundred. Here was the evidence—the southern fur seal had been pushed to the edge of extinction.

But in the four succeeding decades, the fur seal, since protected and left alone, has substantially increased its population. "In South Georgia they now number 300,000, and they are beginning to recolonize the South Orkneys and Shetlands," according to Dr. R. M. Laws of Cambridge, England. Dr. Laws, a leading marine-mammal specialist, estimates that "in another 15 to 20 years the southern fur seal herds may well reach their former abundance."

Unlike fur seals, hair seals have a stiff, coarse pelt. Under their slick skin is a thick layer of blubber that insulates them from the cold. Like all seals, they are sleek and fast-moving in the water, but awkward on top of the ice. Clawing at the hard surface, they hump forward on their short flippers with a caterpillar-like *(Continued on page 188)*

Brittle star, a spiny predator of the Arctic seafloor, slithers quickly along the bottom in search of worms, crustaceans, and small sea urchins. Sometimes called a serpent star, the animal moves by sinuously wriggling its five flexible rays. If the brittle star breaks a ray or loses one in a struggle with another predator, it can grow a replacement.

(Continued on page 188)

Calved by a glacier and sculpted by ocean currents, winds, and the summer sun, a gigantic iceberg plows through waters of the Antarctic—and dwarfs a helicopter. "From a distance icebergs look like graceful marble cliffs or floating castles of alabaster," writes author Joseph B. MacInnis. Huge sheets of ice originating on the Antarctic continent produce thousands of icebergs each year. Some weigh as much as a million tons and measure 100 miles in length. They diminish in size and finally disappear as they drift north toward the tropics. A snow petrel (left), an Antarctic resident throughout the year, pecks at krill swimming in a pool on the surface of an iceberg. The petrel's large eyes help it to find food during the shadowy winter months. Nearly impervious to cold and wind, snow petrels have insulating layers of fat and heavy down beneath thick, overlapping feathers.

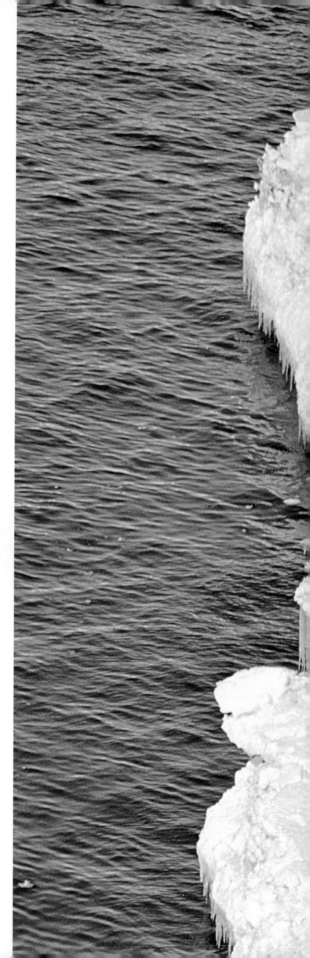

Adélie penguins (right) congregate on
floating pack ice in the Antarctic.
Though flightless, these birds swim with
great proficiency, darting through the
water in pursuit of small crustaceans.
Adult penguins have no enemies on top
of the ice, and act inquisitively when
people approach. In the sea, however,
leopard seals hunt them. Above, a
ten-foot-long leopard seal, named for its
spotted body, humps awkwardly along
the ice after sunning itself. Below,
another leopard seal—a sleek and agile
hunter in the water—eats a penguin.
First it grasped the bird with sharp,
inch-long teeth, and then killed it by
violently shaking it back and forth.

motion. Although seals surface frequently to rest and to sun themselves, they generally look out of place.

Ringed seals are the most numerous of the hair seals at the North Pole, and they once served as the main source of food, fuel, and clothing for the Eskimo.

Many millions of them still winter beneath the six-foot-thick pack ice. To breathe, each ringed seal must keep several holes to the surface open. When ice begins to form and deepen as winter approaches, the seal continually breaks it, gradually forming a vertical tunnel through the pack ice just wide enough for its body. Even though the surface is blanketed by three feet or more of snow, enough air percolates through to keep the seal alive. Because of the importance of these holes, each seal spends a good part of its day keeping its series of air holes clear.

To me the loveliest of all the seals is the crabeater, a hair seal that lives only in the Antarctic. Mature adults are a creamy grayish-white, and their eyes are a haunting brown. A bristling growth of whiskers adds a jauntiness to their demeanor. When they swim, they often break the surface like dolphins, and their slender arched backs glisten with sunlight. The crabeater has not come by its name honestly, however; it actually lives on a diet of krill. To feed, the seal uses its close-fitting teeth as a filter, straining the tiny animals from the water.

If the crabeater is the most beautiful of the seals, the elephant seal is the most outrageous. Males of this species sometimes grow to 6,000 pounds—the largest seals in the world. When angry or threatened, the bull elephant seal inflates his proboscis—a large bladderlike swelling on his face. Air surges into the proboscis and inflates it to the size of a basketball. The seal then produces loud noises ranging from squeaks to growls. The sight of this huge beast, three tons of roaring blubber, is terrifying.

Another of the Antarctic seals is the leopard, a fierce predator of small animals, especially penguins. Named for their brown-spotted bodies, leopard seals have long, sharp teeth for grasping prey. Darting up from below, a leopard seal opens its jaws and slants its teeth into the flesh of a penguin that is swimming on the surface. Then, lashing its long muscular neck back and forth, the leopard seal shakes the penguin to kill it. The seal often bites off the head before eating the body.

One of the world's most unusual birds, the penguin is also one of its finest swimmers. The birds thrust through the water with swift strokes of their flippers, attaining speeds of 15 miles an hour. They leap into and out of the water and can dive to depths of 850 feet or more to find crustaceans. Adult penguins have no predators out of the water, but seabirds eat their eggs and attack their young. The only creature that preys on them in the sea is the leopard seal. There are some 17 species of penguins, but only four that actually live on the Antarctic continent—the emperor, the Adélie, the chinstrap, and the gentoo.

The largest of all penguins, the emperor stands almost four feet tall. In autumn emperors leave the water for the shelf ice and congregate in rookeries of as many as 50,000 birds. There they pair off and mate. A month later each female produces a single one-pound egg. The female then leaves the egg under the supervision of her mate, and heads back to the sea to feed.

For two months, during the harshest part of the Antarctic winter, the male keeps the egg tucked between his feet and his warm abdomen. When the female returns he relinquishes the egg to her and hurries off to feed—he has not eaten since he left the sea three months before.

Soon after he leaves, a small downy chick breaks out of the shell. The mother feeds it by regurgitating food. By summer the chick is mature enough to follow the adults to the sea and begin feeding on its own.

Playful and exuberant, penguins move easily between land and sea. In the Arctic the polar bear also inhabits both worlds—but remains a reclusive and wary animal. Seen from afar, polar bears are pale shadows in a white world—ghosts moving silently across the ice.

From a helicopter I once happened to spot a trio of polar bears—a female followed by two nearly full-grown cubs. They were alone, moving across a large ice floe with an easy, loping gait.

When they heard the approaching helicopter, they picked up speed and began bounding across the thick ice away from our flight path. After a short sprint they came to the edge of the ice floe; the surface of the ocean was coated by a thin rime of recently frozen ice. Without hesitating, they plunged in, scattering ice and water in a silvery spray.

The mother bear, which led the procession through the water, did not swim directly into the thin ice. To avoid its sharp cutting edge, she dove down, swam underwater for a short distance, and then surfaced, shattering the ice like sheet glass. The cubs followed dutifully in her wake. Once they reached another solid floe, the bears clambered up on the ice and shook a spray of water from their muscular bodies. Then they were off, running south as we turned the helicopter north to keep from disturbing them further.

Polar bears are beautifully equipped for such cold-water swimming. They push through the water with powerful strokes of their huge forepaws. They are amply protected from the cold by two layers of fur, a dense, soft undercoat covered by shaggy, oily outer fur. Beneath this warm coat, they carry a thick layer of fat; combined with the fur, it gives the beast an efficient thermal suit.

Polar bears spend much of their lives on the pack ice hunting seals, their favorite prey. They either sneak up on seals that are sunning themselves and crush their skulls with a swat of a large paw or wait for them by their breathing

KJELL B. SANDVED

Swimming with delicate legs, an inch-long amphipod hunts plankton in the Antarctic. These tiny crustaceans form a vital link in the polar food web.

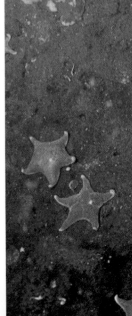

Appendages extended, a rare 12-legged sea spider scurries along the ocean bottom in the Antarctic. Its many legs enable the foot-wide creature to walk, feel, grasp, and eat. Another sea spider and a pair of sea stars (above, right) hunt for food. In a feeding mass (right), spiny-skinned sea stars and several worms compete to devour a dead fish. Ferocious predators, sea stars will attack and eat almost anything their size in the sea. Often they straddle the victim and attach themselves with suction disks on the bottom of their rays. Strong digestive juices from the centrally located stomach dissolve the tissue of the prey. Some species of sea stars can even turn out their stomachs and digest the food before actually swallowing it.

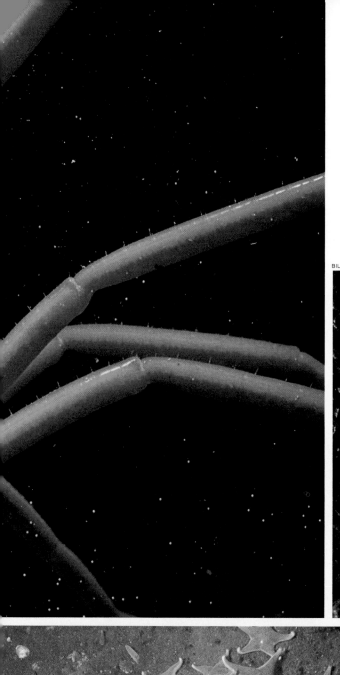

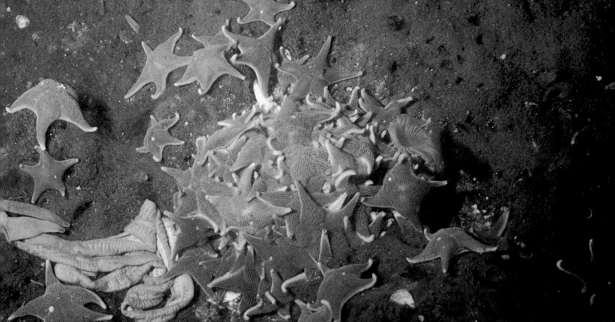

holes. Awesome in both size and ferocity, polar bears weigh as much as 1,500 pounds and can run 25 miles an hour over short distances—fast enough to overtake a man. That is why Eskimos greatly fear the polar bear.

I have often wondered why polar bears, such successful wanderers, are not found in the Antarctic. Seals and ice are plentiful, and survival would not seem to be any more of a problem there than in the Arctic.

The main barrier, of course, is distance. Thousands of miles separate the poles, and the intervening seas are too warm for the polar bear. The only truly successful commuter between the Arctic and the Antarctic is the tiny arctic tern. It

flies some 12,000 miles twice each year to follow summer from polar region to polar region.

Like these small arctic terns, gigantic whales are also great travelers—and despite their bulk, they move with the fluidity and ease of birds. In March 1973 I joined a team of scientists and photographers to follow the migration of bowhead whales along the north shore of Alaska. By incredible good fortune I became the first human being ever to see a bowhead underwater.

We had landed our helicopter at the edge of the ice about 30 miles out in the Chukchi Sea. The water was filled with a dozen or so belugas, small ivory-colored whales that often accompany bowheads.

With great hopes we submerged, but during a half-hour search we found no bowheads. I was swimming just a few feet below the surface, slowly heading back to the helicopter, when I saw a huge dark shape rising from below. It ascended slowly, majestically, to the surface, where with a backward splash of its head, it exhaled a breath that blurred the surroundings. I watched, hypnotized, as the great black animal glided toward me. For a second I tried to imagine what would happen if this 50-ton animal, or its 20-foot-wide tail, brushed me—even gently—against the ice.

Just 20 feet away from me it began to descend. Then, for no apparent reason, it rose again. It passed within inches of me, its great form blacking out the sun. The water between us seemed to hum as it was stirred by the whale's motion. I watched this huge, solid wall of black move past and then slowly begin to descend. I drifted lower with the whale as it swam through a swirling curtain of plankton. In slow motion it dropped deeper into the dark green water and gradually disappeared.

I have seen other whales in other oceans, but this unexpected meeting with a bowhead beneath the free-floating ice of the Chukchi Sea was the most magical encounter I have ever had. I felt that I was in the presence of an animal that symbolized the grandeur of the frozen oceans.

During each of the many dives I have made in polar areas, I have sensed that the importance of the fragment of life I am watching goes beyond the immediately tangible and in some way relates to all life on the globe. Particularly at the North Pole, with the entire world below me, I have envisioned the ocean as a unity, a girdle of water that stretches around the earth, dividing—and yet joining—the continents and the people who dwell on them.

At those times I have felt that we human beings are interwoven into one grand tapestry with every other species of plant and animal life on earth, that our land-based ecosystems merge and become one with the sea-based ecosystems. It is then I clearly understand that people must work to manage and preserve the ocean, to learn that we truly are children of the sea.

Surprised sea lion peers from the water as a southern right whale breaches off the southern coast of Argentina. Patches of calluslike skin, called callosities, encrust the whale, which usually lives far out to sea. Sea lions generally hug the shoreline, spending part of each day on land sunning and resting.

193

Female southern right whale guards her calf from marine biologists approaching in a rubber raft. The 50-foot-long female gave birth to the calf far out at sea, and she will protect it for the first two years of its life. Right whales once numbered in the tens of thousands, but relentless hunting of the creatures for their blubber and whalebone drastically reduced the population. Today only about 4,000 animals survive. A photographer (left) dives with one of the gentle giants: Two mammals—one terrestrial, the other marine—confront each other. Careful study and timely legislation have saved many marine species, including the right whale, from extinction—but many more remain threatened. To protect them and to ensure the continued stability of all life in the sea, man must work to preserve the health and beauty of the wilderness ocean realm.

Authors' Notes

Geologist ROBERT D. BALLARD received his doctorate from the University of Rhode Island and currently works as an Associate Scientist at Woods Hole Oceanographic Institution in Massachusetts. He has contributed three articles on the ocean depths to NATIONAL GEOGRAPHIC.

LINDA McCARTER BRIDGE grew up along the rocky coasts of California, where sailing became a way of life. A freelance journalist, she has written two of the Society's Books for Young Explorers—*Cats: Little Tigers in Your House* and *The Playful Dolphins.*

During childhood vacations near Ocean City, New Jersey, and along the Gulf of Mexico, marine botanist SYLVIA A. EARLE learned to love the sea—and to write about it. Dr. Earle is a Research Scientist and the Curator of Marine Plants at the California Academy of Sciences, and is the Chief Scientist of the Research Vessel *Eagle.*

National Geographic writer TEE LOFTIN holds degrees in journalism from the University of Missouri and American University. Author of the Special Publication *The Wild Shores: America's Beginnings,* she has also written chapters for *Those Inventive Americans, Clues to America's Past,* and *Powers of Nature.*

In recognition of his 20 years studying the relationships between man and the sea, Dr. JOSEPH B. MacINNIS in 1976 was made a Member of the Order of Canada, his nation's highest civilian honor. He is president of Undersea Research Ltd., in Toronto, and has contributed an article on polar diving to NATIONAL GEOGRAPHIC.

Author of the Special Publication *John Muir's Wild America,* TOM MELHAM has also written chapters for *The Craftsman in America* and *Powers of Nature.* A graduate of Cornell University, he received a master's degree in journalism from the University of Missouri. He joined the staff of the Society in 1971.

H. ROBERT MORRISON, Managing Editor for National Geographic Educational Filmstrips, contributed a chapter to the Special Publication *As We Live and Breathe: The Challenge of Our Environment.* He joined the Society's staff in 1964, became a certified diver for this book, and continues to dive as a hobby.

Additional Reading

Isobel Bennett, *The Great Barrier Reef;* Archie Carr, *So Excellent A Fishe* and *The Everglades;* Margaret Deacon, *Scientists and the Sea;* N. C. Flemming, ed., *The Undersea;* Hans W. Fricke, *The Coral Seas;* Sir Alister C. Hardy, *Fish & Fisheries* and *Great Waters* and *The Open Sea;* Bayard H. McConnaughey, *Introduction to Marine Biology;* Richard Perry, *The Polar Worlds;* Edward F. Ricketts and Jack Calvin, *Between Pacific Tides;* Carl Roessler, *The Underwater Wilderness—Life Around the Great Reefs;* David A. Ross, *Introduction to Oceanography;* Sir Frederick S. Russell and Sir Maurice Yonge, *The Seas;* H. U. Sverdrup, Martin W. Johnson, and Richard H. Fleming, *The Oceans;* John and Mildred Teal, *Life and Death of the Salt Marsh* and *The Sargasso Sea;* Ian Thornton, *Darwin's Islands;* Alywne Wheeler, *Fishes of the World.* National Geographic Special Publications: *World Beneath the Sea* and *Undersea Treasures.*

In NATIONAL GEOGRAPHIC: Robert D. Ballard, "Window on Earth's Interior," August 1976; William Beebe, "A Half Mile Down," December 1934; Eugenie Clark, "The Strangest Sea," September 1975; John B. Corliss and Robert D. Ballard, "Oases of Life in the Cold Abyss," October 1977; Rick Gore, "The Tree Nobody Liked," May 1977; William Graves, "The Imperiled Giants," December 1976; J. R. Heirtzler and Robert D. Ballard, "Project FAMOUS—Man's First Voyages Down to the Mid-Atlantic Ridge," May 1975; Stephen W. Hitchcock, "Can We Save Our Salt Marshes?" June 1972; Joseph B. MacInnis, "Diving Beneath Arctic Ice," August 1973; Kenneth MacLeish, "Australia's Great Barrier Reef," June 1973; Samuel W. Matthews, "Antarctica's Nearer Side," November 1971; Wheeler J. North, "Giant Kelp, Sequoias of the Sea," August 1972. Readers may also wish to consult the *National Geographic Index* for related material.

DAVID DOUBILET

Clustered school of sweepers hovers in a coral cave as a diver descends a reef in the Red Sea.

Acknowledgments

The Special Publications Division is grateful to the individuals, organizations, and agencies named or quoted in the text and to those cited here for their generous cooperation and assistance during the preparation of this book: Dr. Theodore R. Dudley, Harold J. Egoscue, Dr. Richard W. Grigg, Thomas J. Kelly, Dr. John E. Randall, Dr. John W. Wells, and Dr. Warren Zyler; American Museum of Natural History, National Marine Fisheries Service, National Science Foundation, Scripps Institute of Oceanography, Smithsonian Institution, U. S. Fish and Wildlife Service, Woods Hole Oceanographic Institution.

Index

Library of Congress CIP Data
The Ocean Realm.
Bibliography p.196; Includes index
1. Underwater exploration. 2. Marine Biology.
I. National Geographic Society, Washington, D. C., Special Publications Division.
GC65.026   500.9'162   77-93399
ISBN 0-87044-251-1

Composition for *The Ocean Realm* by National Geographic's Photographic Services, Carl M. Shrader, Chief; Lawrence F. Ludwig, Assistant Chief. Printed and bound by Kingsport Press, Kingsport, Tenn. Color separations by Colorgraphics, Inc., Forestville, Md.; Graphic South, Charlotte, N.C.; National Bickford Graphics, Inc., Providence, R.I.; Progressive Color Corp., Rockville, Md.; J. Wm. Reed Co., Alexandria, Va.

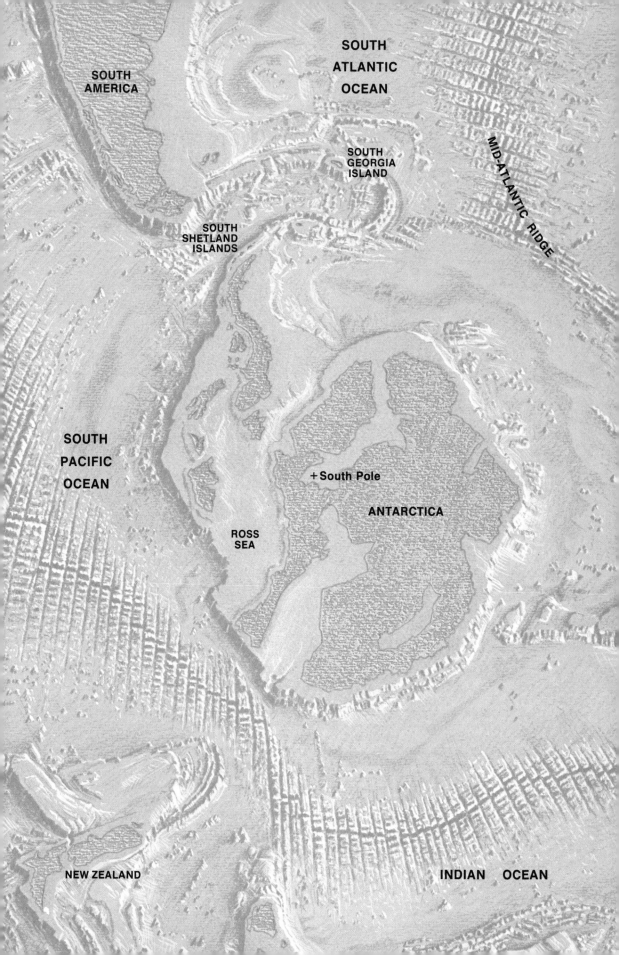

SOUTH
AMERICA

SOUTH
ATLANTIC
OCEAN

SOUTH
GEORGIA
ISLAND

MID-ATLANTIC RIDGE

SOUTH
SHETLAND
ISLANDS

SOUTH
PACIFIC
OCEAN

+South Pole

ANTARCTICA

ROSS
SEA

NEW ZEALAND

INDIAN   OCEAN

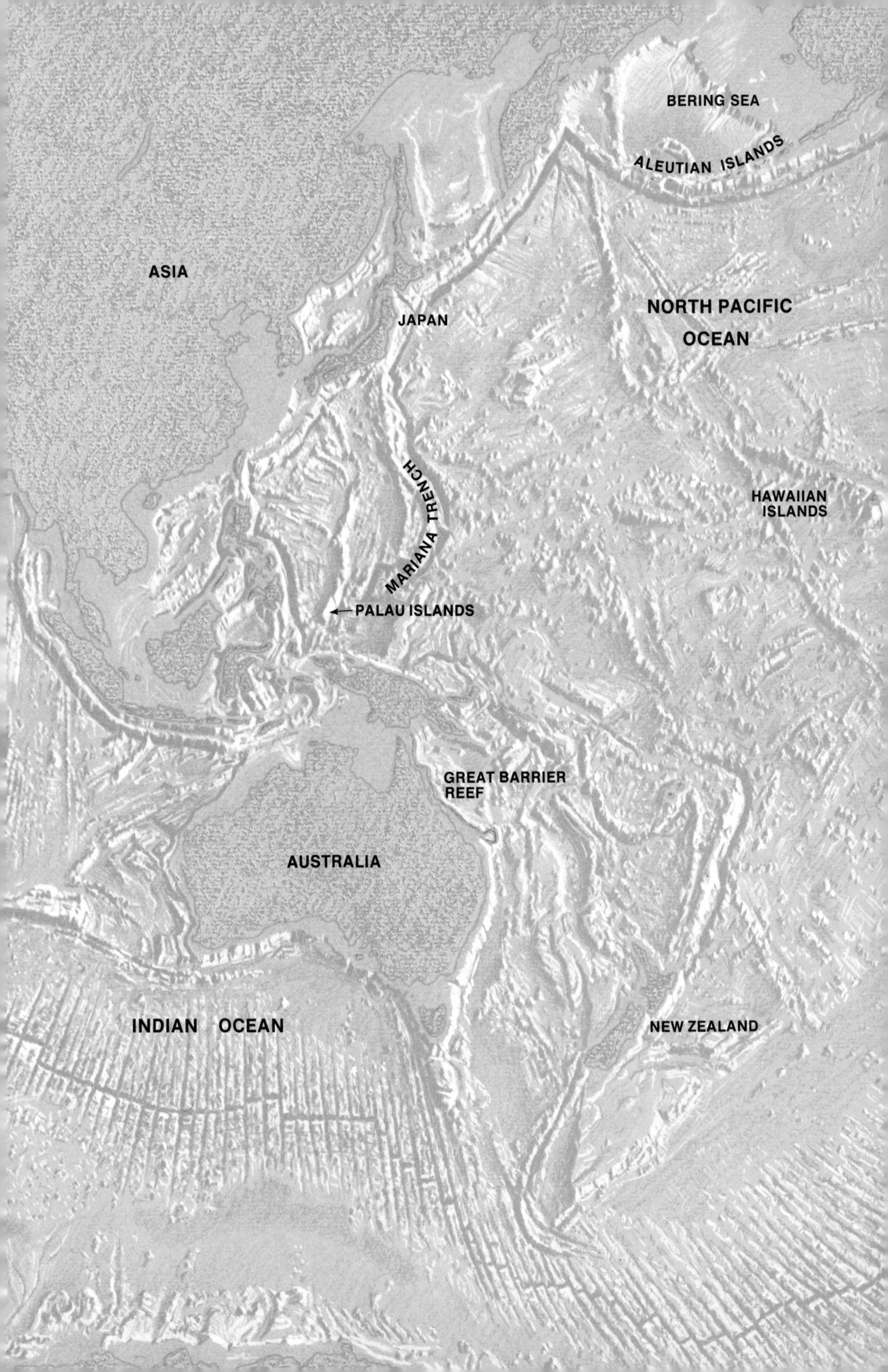
BERING SEA
ALEUTIAN ISLANDS
ASIA
JAPAN
NORTH PACIFIC OCEAN
MARIANA TRENCH
HAWAIIAN ISLANDS
PALAU ISLANDS
GREAT BARRIER REEF
AUSTRALIA
INDIAN OCEAN
NEW ZEALAND